forgiveness
opens the heart
to Gods Blessing

Love
Sarah

CHOOSING TO
FORGIVE
LEARNING TO
LOVE

CHOOSING TO
FORGIVE
LEARNING TO
LOVE

SARAH MCCLEARY

Pleasant Word
A Division of WinePress Group
PW

Pleasant Word (a division of WinePress Publishing, PO Box 428, Enumclaw, WA 98022) functions only as book publisher. As such, the ultimate design, content, editorial accuracy, and views expressed or implied in this work are those of the author.

ISBN 13: 978-1-4141-0738-7
ISBN 10: 1-4141-0738-2
Library of Congress Catalog Card Number: 2008911838

CONTENTS

THANK YOU

THANK YOU TO my aunt and uncle, for accepting me as your daughter, for the love and sacrifices of raising another child, and for giving me everything you possibly could and then some.

To my brothers, thank you for accepting me as a sister and looking out for me.

I thank God for all the times that He carried me through and for everyone He placed in my path to help me through this journey to a place of healing.

To all the people that I hurt along the way, "Forgive me, for I knew not," and to the sister that I have hated for 37 years, I forgive you.

Chapter One

CHOICES

ONE MIGHT SAY that the sum of our lives is made up of the choices we make. Some of our choices are wise, and some are foolish. Some of our choices may seem good at the time but, in retrospect, we wish we could take them back. It's the same with forgiveness. It's a choice we make, and making that decision is half the battle.

Thank you for choosing to come along with me on a journey of discovering the power of forgiveness and love. It was through this journey that I came to learn that forgiveness is a choice. And as a result of choosing to forgive, I learned how to love. Most of us think that we should already know how to do these things, right? It's simple! But sometimes things happen, and we get lost. We get broken. Oftentimes, we don't even realize that there's something wrong. I know that I didn't until God opened my eyes to what was binding me so tight that I could hardly breathe.

You'll see in my story that my pain was hidden so deep that it became a part of me. Most of my actions and reactions were based on me being a prisoner to an invisible force (a deeply rooted hurt) that I didn't understand or realize existed. In some cases, I caused my own hurts by the foolish choices that I made.

One day, I took a hard look at the image in the mirror and realized that I didn't like the person who was looking back at me. Imagine looking through the doorway to the human soul and following a path that leads to the center of the heart, the root of all things, good and evil. I saw a heart that was heavy from the weight of bitterness and unforgiveness. I saw a heart whose hurts had been buried for so long that a brick wall had formed around it. Nothing and no one could get through that wall, including the love of God. Like the children of Israel, I had been wandering lost in the desert for years. Now that I'm on the road to my destiny, I just can't stop praising Him for the things He has done.

It's been said that you can't teach an old dog new tricks, but I don't believe that. I think all that is required are three simple things: (1) having a desire to change, (2) having faith that you will change, and (3) refocusing your thoughts. As I explored who I was and who I wanted to be, I realized that my life was empty, even with all of the people around me. I was angry and had a self-defeating attitude. I grumbled and complained, and I had actually convinced myself that I didn't deserve to be happy. I lacked gratitude and didn't trust anyone.

As I examined my life and how I had arrived at this place, I began to realize that the root of all these unwanted characteristics had come from being abandoned as a child and not dealing with it. I wanted to heal; I wanted to fix myself. I wanted to let go of the hurt, the pain and the wrongful thinking that I had developed over the past thirty-seven years.

Isaiah 53:5 says that by His stripes we are healed. I took a deeper look and found that this Scripture didn't just apply to my physical pain but to my emotional pain as well. As I sought to understand what was really going on within me, I remembered Paul's words in Ephesians 6:12: "For we wrestle not against flesh and blood, but against principalities, against powers, against the rulers of the darkness of this world, against spiritual wickedness in high places." As I studied this verse, I realized that the war was going on in my own mind! I was at war with myself. I realized that I couldn't live until I had forgiven those who had hurt me.

Forgiving others meant that I had to give up the right I had always thought I had to punish those who had hurt me. It meant that I had to put the past behind me and fully let go and pardon those who had offended me. As Paul writes in Philippians 3:13, "Brethren, I do not count myself to have apprehended; but one thing I do, *forgetting those things which are behind* and reaching forward to those things which are ahead" (Italics added). I also realized that in order to move forward, I had to change how I thought. I had to renew my mind. As Paul states in Romans 12:2, "Do not conform any longer to the pattern of this world, but *be transformed by the renewing of your mind*" (Italics added).

The result was a freedom I thought I'd never experience. I was able to let down the walls and trust in the Lord with all my heart and soul. I was able to let the love of God in, and He has given me that deep-down happiness that lives inside of me no matter what. And as the old way of life was cut away and the new life reborn, God placed a desire in my heart to share my story so that it might help others experience their own rebirth.

In this book, I have been surprisingly candid about the mistakes I've made and the lessons I've learned in order to show you how God has transformed my life. Through His Grace—His power and anointing on my life—I have experienced a victory that has changed me forever and put me on a path to a new beginning. As I grow in my relationship with God, I've experienced a peace I can't explain.

God has extended this same grace to everyone, but it's *our* choice to accept it or reject it. I encourage you to view this time as a new beginning. It is important that you begin by making the choice to adopt a "can do" attitude. Once you make up your mind and believe that you can change, God will do the rest. You will feel the power of the Holy Spirit begin to work inside of you to destroy the things that bind you. You will experience the freedom of letting go of your past hurts and pains and begin to move forward through the healing of your heart and the renewing of your mind. You will begin to heal, and your anger, heaviness and hardness of heart will fade away.

As you read my testimony in the following chapters, be transparent with yourself. As you explore your own hurts, use the space in the margins to make notes for yourself. Brace yourself for an eye-opening experience. It takes courage to be truthful with yourself and it may be painful. As things come to mind regarding events or situations in your past that you haven't fully dealt with or people whom you haven't released because of hurts they may have caused you, write them down.

It's important for us to remember to forgive ourselves for the mistakes and wrong decisions we've made in our lives. In Romans 8:1, Paul says, "There is, therefore, now no condemnation for those who are in Christ Jesus." So if God doesn't remember our sin, why should we beat ourselves up over the mistakes we've made or the hurts that others have caused us? I was black and blue from replaying my mistakes over and over again, but I learned to let go of the negative voice in my head that kept reminding me of my failures. So those people who hurt you and you can't remember why, it's time to let it go. That chip on your shoulder, it's time to let it go. It's time for a new beginning.

After you read my testimony, you will begin your journey to the road of forgiveness through fasting and meditating on the Word of God. I know what you are thinking: *Fasting? I don't want to do that. It requires giving up something!* Yes, you are right, you will have to give up something: your anger, your bad attitudes, your insecurities, your disappointments and your pain. For me, the paralyzing effect of abandonment was the feeling of being rejected and alone. I felt that I wasn't wanted and wasn't loved. It was through fasting—not eating certain foods, abstaining from wrong thoughts, and spending dedicated time with God—that I began to be able to forgive the ones who had abandoned me. As a result, my heart was opened to a new kind of love.

Being in a position to receive allowed me to open my heart to how much God loved me and see how perfect His love was for me. Through His love, I realized that I am never alone, for He walks with me each and every day. I was freed from the voices of fear and doubt—from the voices telling me that I would never amount to anything and that no one would ever love me. At the end of my fast, I was no longer consumed with seeking love from my sister and others, for God's Word had captured my heart.

Each day during the fast, you will have a scripture or positive message to read and a short exercise to complete. Allow some quiet time to meditate as you work through the exercises, and be transparent with yourself and God (He already knows anyway) so that you can experience full victory and freedom in Christ as I did.

I pray that this book will provide inspiration to transform your life the way it has transformed mine, that it will bring you to a place of peace and love that can only be found in God, and that at the end of your journey you will be able to perceive the new thing that God has been doing. In Him, I've found the love I've longed for—an unconditional love and a supernatural peace that is beyond human understanding. I will be praying for you, and I invite you to drop me a line to share your journey.

Chapter Two

DISCOVERING THE BITTER ROOT

AS MY FRIEND Martha and I drove to worship service, we listened to the *Rebirth of Kirk Franklin* CD and talked about the introduction on track 1. On that opening track, a woman is depicted as leaving her child to the care of his grandmother. Martha felt that the introduction was the best part of the CD, but I hated it. When she listened to the introduction, she heard the dedication of the child to the Lord. When I heard it, it reminded me of stories I'd heard on the news about mothers who, feeling that there was no way out, had left their children on a doorstep.

The next day, I listened to the words of the introduction over and over again. Each time I heard something different. The child crying, longing to stay with his mother, wanting to go home. I could picture the child, not wanting his mother to leave him, screaming in agony as his mother handed him over to his grandmother. From the dialogue, I imagined it wasn't the first time that she had left him. I sympathized with the child and felt his pain; his desire to just belong and be with his mother. Then it hit me. The reason I hated the introduction so much and imagined all these negative thoughts was because it reminded me of *me*! It was what I had felt growing up: being left behind, not understanding why, and longing for my family.

I remember sitting in a church at the age of six and seeing my mother lying in front of me in a box. I didn't understand that she had passed away and I would never see her again. Three weeks later, there I was again sitting in the church—this time it was my father lying in a box. A few weeks after that, it was my grandmother. Then my older sister walked on out me, and I never saw her again. I don't remember her saying goodbye or lying in a box like the others.

It was at this young age, that the trauma and feelings of abandonment I experienced began to define me and fill my heart with such bitterness that it would take years to heal. I withdrew into my own quiet world and kept my struggles and pains hidden from everyone. Although I had the opportunity to do so, I didn't talk with anyone about what was going on. No one knew the wrong images and hatred that were hardening my heart.

Through the innocence of my childhood, I had developed an unrealistic dream of what a family was supposed to be. For me, it meant having my mother, father and my big sister around me all the time.

It meant being a part of something and belonging to a group. It meant having someone to protect me when I was afraid so that I could feel safe. It meant having someone to care for me, to hug and kiss me and wipe my tears away. To me, family was about the laughter joy and on the bad days, having someone there to count on no matter what.

Family relationships are important to our social and emotional growth. They provide us with a foundation of who we are as children and who we will grow up to be. Our families teach us about love, beliefs, and values and guide us through those critical development stages of our lives.

At the time I suffered this loss, emotionally I was at the stage of developing confidence and self-esteem and learning to trust. I was beginning to form my own opinions, likes, and dislikes. Socially, I was learning about acceptance and how to interact with others. As a child, my days should have been carefree and filled with play dates, dresses, dolls and ice cream. But then everything I knew was ripped out from under me, leaving me feeling empty and gutted like a fish.

My hurt was so deep that in order to survive, I buried that hurt deep within my heart where no one else was allowed. I completely erased everything else from my mind and pretended that the traumatic events of my childhood had never happened. That's how I survived. I closed myself off from the pain, because I thought that would protect me from the hurt that was consuming me.

In Hebrews 12:15, we read, "It is written...see to it that no one misses the grace of God and that no bitter root grows up to cause trouble and defile many." By burying my pain and disappointment and pretending that my loss never happened, I actually allowed that pain to grab hold in my life and take root, and that bitter root caused my heart to become resentful. Little did I know it at the time, but that pain and resentment wouldn't stay buried. My hurt, remained dormant for a while, poisoning me on the inside. It was like a bomb just waiting to explode. And when it did explode, it caused a lot of pain in my life and in the lives others. It left a path of destruction and strongholds in my life that only the love of God could break.

In John 10:9-11, Jesus says that the thief comes only to steal and kill and destroy, but that He has come that others may have life and have it to the full. When we allow bitterness and resentment to control us, it opens the door for the enemy to steal, kill and destroy. It causes us to lose our hopes, dreams, families, finances and relationships.

I believe that each of us have a path we must walk. Each of us must make a choice to follow the path that God has for us and embark on a journey of spiritual growth so that we can become the people we are destined to be. It's a journey to find the full life that God has for us. But it is not an easy journey. Because of God's permissive will—and sometimes as a result of our own disobedience and poor choices—He allows (and sometimes sends) tests and trials our way. Most of the time, these tests and trials are intended to help us grow closer in our relationship with God. As we learn from these trials, we are cleansed of unwanted characteristics that are not of Christ and learn to trust that God will see us through. Our trials give us a testimony and are used to develop our faith. However, if we let them, these tests and trials can cause us to become bitter and resentful.

I've grown to view the Bible as a practical guide to life, and I've found that it contains the answer to just about any trial we will ever face. One of the things I've discovered in reading Scripture is that Satan has to get permission from God in order to test us. Again, sometimes we bring these trials on ourselves as a result of not being obedient to God's will and by making poor decisions. But God is faithful and just and will see us through (even in spite of ourselves).

In Luke 22:31-34, Jesus told Peter that Satan had asked to sift him like wheat. He then told Peter he would deny Him three times before the rooster crowed that day (see also John 13:36-38). In Peter's mind, he was a loyal and faithful follower. He was so sure of his loyalty that he was willing to go to prison and die for Jesus. But little did he know that a trial was about come upon him that would expose his weakness and fear. After Jesus had been arrested and taken before the high priest, a servant girl accused Peter of being one of Jesus' followers. Upon questioning, Peter responded, "Woman, I don't know him" (Luke 22:57). When faced with the possibility of death, Peter became afraid and denied knowing Jesus.

However, Peter later went on to become a valuable warrior for the Lord, changing the course of his life and the lives of others. How was he able to prevent his failure during his time of trial from getting the best of him and leading him down a path of defeat? If you continue to read the story in Luke, you will find the key: "Then Peter remembered the word the Lord had spoken to him…and he went outside and wept bitterly" (Luke 22:61-62). Peter repented for what he had done. To "repent" means to turn from our old ways and turn back to God. So, from this example we see that when we make mistakes, we should learn from them, change our course and move forward.

Let's look at a second example from the book of Job. Again, Satan first had to get permission from God before he could bring any trials upon Job.

> One day the angels came to present themselves before the LORD and Satan also came with them. The LORD said to Satan, "Where have you come from?" Satan answered the LORD, "From roaming through the earth and going back and forth in it." Then the LORD said to Satan, "Have you considered my servant Job? There is no one on earth like him; he is blameless and upright, a man who fears God and shuns evil." "Does Job fear God for nothing?" Satan replied. "Have you not put a hedge around him and his household

and everything he has? You have blessed the work of his hands, so that his flocks and herds are spread throughout the land. But stretch out your hand and strike everything he has and he will surely curse you to your face." The LORD said to Satan, "Very well, then, everything he has is in your hands, but on the man himself do not lay a finger."

—Job 1:6-12

Job suffered loss after loss. His family, his livestock and his home were taken away, yet he refused to question God. He said, "The LORD gave and the LORD has taken away; may the name of the LORD be praised" (Job 1:21). (Now, it is important to understand from this comment that while God had allowed these trials to occur, it was Satan who had stolen from Job, not God.) Later, we read that Job loses his health, but still he refuses to curse God and sin. I love his response in Job 2:10: "Shall we accept good from God, and not trouble?" The Bible tells us that we can expect difficulties from time to time throughout our lives. It is how we respond to these difficulties that defines us as individuals and our relationship with God.

I've started keeping a list of all the things that God has done for me so that when trouble comes I can reflect on His blessings. I find that focusing on the positive instead of the negative helps to keep me moving forward instead of staying stuck in the negative situation.

Even Jesus Christ Himself had to endure trials and temptation. In Luke 4:1-11, we read the following story:

Then Jesus was led by the Spirit into the desert to be tempted by the devil. After fasting forty days and forty nights, he was hungry. The tempter came to him and said, "If you are the Son of God, tell these stones to become bread." Jesus answered, "It is written: 'Man does not live on bread alone, but on every word that comes from the mouth of God.'" Then the devil took him to the holy city and had him stand on the highest point of the temple. "If you are the Son of God," he said, "throw yourself down. For it is written: 'He will command his angels concerning you, and they will lift you up in their hands, so that you will not strike your foot against a stone.'" Jesus answered him, "It is also written: 'Do not put the Lord your God to the test.'" Again, the devil took him to a very high mountain and showed him all the kingdoms of the world and their splendor. "All this I will give you," he said, "if you will bow down and worship me." Jesus said to him, "Away from me, Satan! For it is written: 'Worship the Lord your God, and serve him only.'" Then the devil left him and angels came and attended him.

Notice that each time Jesus was tempted, He applied the Word of God to His situation and counteracted Satan's attack. Satan had no effect on him. James

4:7 says, "Submit yourselves, then, to God. Resist the devil, and he will flee from you." Through the power of the Holy Spirit, we can resist the devil, and he will flee. We have to constantly be on guard against anything that influences us negatively or is in any way contrary to God's Word. So it is important for us to keep our hearts free from toxic waste. As we make the choice to resist the opportunity to be proud, to hurt someone, to repay evil with evil or to stand and not be moved, temptation will flee from us.

I have learned from my own experience that when we make the decision to fully give our lives to God, Satan will do everything he can to stop us from being used by God. As we learn to press through the difficulties of life, our testimony to God's power to keep and deliver us from whatever obstacle we face is strengthened. (God has said that He is The Great I AM and that whatever our need, He is the answer.) Our experiences cause our personal testimonies to become more fruitful, because it's born out of obedience and suffering in the name of Jesus.

It's unfortunate that we live in a world in which violence and hatred is so widespread, but God is able to turn every circumstance around for good. That is what he did for me. He delivered me from the emotional bondage that I had lived in for years.

As I wrote this book, I constantly sought the Lord and asked, "Who am I, Lord, to write a book on forgiveness?"

After all, it took me thirty-seven years to let my bitterness go, and I am still constantly reminded of my past. How can I help someone who has not let his or her past go and forgiven? Then I remembered Jesus' words in Matthew 7:3: "Why do you look at the speck of sawdust in your brother's eye and pay no attention to the plank in your own eye? You hypocrite, first take the plank out of your own eye, and then you will see clearly to remove the speck from your brother's eye." Now that God has removed the speck from my eye and the hardness from heart (ouch and it was a painful process!), I am a new creature. The old has gone, and the new is emerging. I say "emerging" because I have not yet arrived at my final destination, but I can perceive the new thing that God is doing in my life and continue to press forward. Now that I am a new creature in Christ, I want to share my story so that I can bless others.

The idea for this book came to me several years ago, but it took me a long time to bring this writing to life because I doubted I would have the courage to share my trials. During the course of writing this book, I stopped several times. I had to keep telling myself that I can do all things through Christ who strengthens me (see Philippians 4:13) and that God wouldn't give me a task without giving me the ability to complete it. I also worried about how this book would affect lives—primarily the lives of those God had entrusted me to. But then I realized that this book is not about them (names of the characters in this book have been given biblical names). It's about God's healing power in my life and how He healed me in spirit, mind and soul. Through that healing, I learned about true love.

I don't know why God chose to take my parents when He did or why He allowed my sister to walk away. But as I've grown up, I've discovered that I don't have a need to understand why anymore. So while I still don't understand it, I thank God for providing me with a new family who gave me a wonderful home with everything I needed and most of what I wanted.

Many of us have allowed our circumstances to limit us. If we would admit it, we've held on to our pain, letting it rob us of our joy and the blessings that God has for us. In my own life, I didn't recognize what was going on inside of me or that this pain had taken root so deeply. Because I was so quiet as a child, my family was not aware of my battles. I never talked to anyone about how I felt. No one was aware of the anger, the wrong self-image, the doubt, the fear, the voices or the wall that was growing within me. So again, I say to you that it was a quite a struggle.

I know from experience that emotional scars hurt, so I won't tell you to get over it. Rather, I want to share my experience of triumph through my relationship with God in the hope that it might lead you to want to know Him for yourself. For it was God's love that surrounded me and brought me through my pain. So many of us have put bandages on our wounds to stop the bleeding but have never treated the wound. So I invite you to take off the bandage, the temporary fix, and be healed and made whole.

I don't consider myself an authoritative expert on the subject. I'm just an ordinary person, and it has been a long road to freedom for me. But as I read the Bible, I began to notice how God used ordinary people to accomplish His will. Take Noah, for example, who had no idea how to build an ark. Gideon was the lowest in his family and had no idea how to lead an army. Then there was the shepherd boy David, who slew and defeated a giant. God transformed each of them and used them according to His purpose.

Look at the lives of the disciples. They were fishermen, tent builders, carpenters and teachers, but they all had one thing in common: a willing spirit. The apostle Paul persecuted Christians. But one day on the road to Damascus, he met Jesus and his life was changed forever. When Paul was later imprisoned, he didn't complain about his bondage but instead used his time in prison to advance the gospel. The Bible is full of examples of people who overcame life's struggles. It is a roadmap for how we should handle life's obstacles.

Let us not forget the people in today's world whom God is using to touch lives. People like Donnie McClurkin, who overcame his past (read *The Donnie McClurkin Story*) and freely lives his life with transparency so that others might know what God has done in his life. What makes such modern-day disciples special is that they are willing to tell their stories so that God can use their lives to bring healing to others. They are willing to share the darkness of their lives so that others may live in the light. They live their lives transparently so that those who are facing similar situations can know that they are not the only ones who face such trials.

No matter what race or gender we are, we all have hurts that we've tried to leave behind. We are all in need of healing in some area of our lives, but we have to stop holding on to the past. We hold on because we think it will keep us from being hurt again, but holding on to the hurt only causes us more pain. We have to let the brick wall down so that God can come in and heal us.

God has taken my struggle and turned it into a calling so that I might help others forgive the hurts they have endured. So it is with a humbled heart that I accept the call to be used to do God's work by the sharing of the joys and pains of my trials. My prayer is that my story may help others to heal and not waste years of their lives on bitterness and unforgiveness, as I did. It is my desire that they will be set free and that they will experience their own miracle of healing through the presence of the Lord. For it is God's presence that moved me to a place of peace, and I know that He can and will do the same for others.

Chapter Three

THE BEGINNING OF THE END

IT WAS THURSDAY afternoon, and I had left work forty-five minutes early to go home and recoup from a bad day. Little did I know that my bad day was just beginning. I lay down, took a deep breath and began to drift off to sleep, only to be awakened by the phone. It was the police.

"Are you Sarah?" They asked.

"Yes," I replied.

"Would you mind stepping outside?"

"Okay." I went outside, but no one was there.

"Are you outside?" the policeman said.

"Yes," I replied, "I am."

"We don't see you."

"I don't see you either."

"What is your address?"

"635 Rodeo Drive."

Realizing they had gone to my old address, the policeman asked me to stay on the phone and wait outside while they drove to my new address which was three miles away. So I did. My heart bounded in fear as I sat on the front porch and wondered what was going on.

A few minutes later, four police cars and an ambulance pulled up. It looked like a scene out of a bad movie. *This is crazy,* I thought. *Why all of this for one 140-pound woman? What could I have done?* Four policemen walked up my driveway while four others stood next to the ambulance and talked to each other.

"What's going on?" I asked.

"We received a call that someone at this address was threatening to kill herself." I thought—no, I *knew*—that they were crazy. After all, as a child, I hadn't been nicknamed "chicken" for nothing! Me? Hurt myself? I wasn't into pain.

I had to pinch myself, because I thought I was dreaming. I pictured my story appearing on the 10 o'clock news. I imagined the news anchor saying, "A woman has been shot on her front porch by police, who thought they saw a gun." I kept telling myself not to move; not to give them an excuse to shoot me.

"Do you own a gun?" one of the officers said.

"Yes," I replied.

"Do you have it on you?"

"It's in the house." The officers could sense the confusion I was feeling. After talking with me for a few minutes, they could see that I wasn't a real threat, so only two officers entered the house with me. As we walked in, they me asked if anyone else was home with me. I told them no and that the gun was upstairs. They followed me into the upstairs bedroom, and I opened the drawer where I kept the gun. It wasn't loaded, so I also picked up the clip. Even though the officers didn't have a search warrant, I handed the gun over to them. I didn't want them to obtain a warrant and come back while I wasn't there and trash the place looking for it.

I had just moved into this house—my first single-family home—earlier that week. It was a small twenty-year old house that needed a lot of work, but it was mine. No more condo fees. One of the first things I did after I moved in was to call a locksmith to change the locks. He put in the new locks, but to my surprise, when I tested one by turning it to the lock position and pulling on it, it opened.

I questioned the locksmith about this and asked him why the door opened when it should have stayed closed. I explained that as a woman living alone, I didn't feel safe with the door being able to open like that. If I pulled on a door when it was locked, I wanted to know that it wouldn't open!

The locksmith explained that this was part of a new safety law. This was the type of lock his company was now installing because of all the recent fires and people getting locked in the stairwells. This lock was designed to open from the inside, even if it was in the locked position. I understood his company's position, but I told him that I still wanted the old style of lock to be put in. I could see the rationale of installing this type of lock in a high-rise building, commercial property or the home for the elderly, but not mine. I felt that the locksmith should have asked me what type of lock I wanted installed before he just put one in.

I was unhappy with the work the locksmith had performed and wanted to have the locks changed to ones that made me feel more secure. I called two other locksmiths, and they told me that they had not heard of the ordinance. So I called the owner of the company for the first locksmith. He was rude to me, so I did what any consumer would have done when he or she wasn't happy with a service: I put a hold on the check.

The owner soon sent me a letter threatening to take me to court. I called to reason with him, explaining that all I wanted was to have my locks changed. When I spoke with his secretary, she told me that the owner had filed a lawsuit against me and went on and on about it.

"I'm the one out money," I said. "I could kill this guy." In hindsight, I shouldn't have made this comment to her. The 911 attacks were still recent, and we were now living in the new homeland security era.

The secretary immediately called the police and told them that I had threatened her and that she was afraid. I couldn't help but wonder how much of this had to do with race. Me, an African American, saying I wanted to kill a white man. It was a figure of speech that people used all the time. When I made the comment, I wasn't yelling, nor was I upset. It was innocent, but she called the police and sent them to my house anyway.

So now, here I was handing the gun my uncle had given me over to the two officers who had entered my home. When the officers followed me back downstairs, I explained what happened. They said that because a report had been filed, it was procedure for me to go with them. I asked if I could get my purse and keys, and they said okay. I gathered my things and turned the alarm on.

Back outside, the neighbors began to gather. I just kept my head down as the officer asked me to step into the ambulance. The paramedics took me to a nearby hospital. On the ride over, I kept thinking, *This isn't real; this isn't happening*. I sat there in silence with paramedics on both sides of me. I didn't know what else to do but lower my head and pray. I totally surrendered myself to the Lord, asking for His help. I didn't know what was going to happen. I was scared. Would I be arrested for the innocent comment I had made—an innocent comment that had been taken out of context and had now gone too far? I was in a situation in which I was totally dependent on God to see me through.

As I prayed that God would remove me from this situation, I thought of the commandment "you shall not murder" in the Ten Commandments (Exodus 20:13) and Jesus' words in Matthew 5:21: "Do not murder." It was just a thought! It was a thought I had often during an argument or when I was angry with someone, but I never took it any further than that.

Over the course of my life, I've observed that thoughts that are not in alignment with the Word of God, or destructive thoughts that go *unchecked,* have the potential to turn into action if we continue to focus on them. I've learned that this is how Satan has gotten his opportunities with me. Once the seed is sown—a thought is planted—and I allow the voice of anger, fear, doubt or rage to take over, Satan is able to get a foothold and gain entrance in my life. The more I focus on the situation, the more I am drawn in. I become Satan's puppet.

I've even thought about killing myself from time to time, but again, this was only a thought—and usually when I had made a huge mistake or was feeling sorry for myself. I imagine a lot of people have had these types of thoughts in passing after they realized they made a huge mistake. But one thing I always knew was that no matter how bad the situation, God was bigger than any problem or mistake I could ever make. So for me, it was only a thought that passed through my mind. Okay, maybe the thought stayed with me for a day or two, if it was a really big mistake. But after I stopped focusing on the mistake and stopped feeling sorry for myself, that thought went away.

If we focus on our thoughts too long, we are likely to eventually act on them. That is why we have to constantly take a stand against the negative thoughts that we know are destructive and not of God. I once heard a speaker mention putting our thoughts in check by asking ourselves, *Is this thought true? Is it necessary? Will it harm anyone?* As I have matured, I have tried to follow this practice whenever a negative comment came into my mind that I was tempted to make. While the comment might have passed the first test and been true, it didn't pass the second or third: It wasn't necessary, and it would hurt someone. I'm now learning to keep a guard over my tongue. It's not necessary to make a comment that will hurt someone, even if it is true.

As we got closer to the hospital, I began to bargain with God. Now, I want to make it clear that in my infancy stages of my relationship with God, I thought I could bargain with Him. But as I've grown into a more mature relationship with God, I have come to realize—and want you to understand—that there is no bargaining with God. Because of His great love for us, He blesses us freely according to His will. But, as I said, at that time in my life I didn't understand that. So I said, "God, if You get me out of this situation, I will do whatever You ask." He had my full attention now, and it was in this moment of weakness that I realized there was nothing I could do within my own strength. I was helpless.

As I sat there, I thought about the request my uncle had asked of me to one day contact my sister—the same sister who had walked away when I was six years old, never to be heard from again. He knew that she had hurt me more than words could ever describe, but he also felt it was his duty to reconcile us. He had sacrificed so much for me that I felt I would do anything for him. He had given me all he could to make sure I had a safe home and an education. So, sitting there in the ambulance, I decided that if I got out of this mess, I would honor his request.

There was something about being in a situation like this that made me feel as if I were running out of time. It was time to put my life in order. Besides, in my heart, I had never forgotten my sister. Even though I couldn't understand how she could walk away, deep inside I still loved her. I would never admit it, but I did still love her, and I hadn't stopped wondering why she had left.

When we arrived at the hospital, I was taken to an exam room. As I sat there, I could hear the policemen explaining to the doctors outside the exam room what had happened. Moments later, several doctors and nurses began coming in and out. One doctor asked, "Do you want to hurt yourself"? Another doctor asked, "Is anyone causing you harm? Would you like to talk with someone?" I was upset, but I knew it wouldn't help the situation. It was humiliating, to say the least, but I tried to remain calm and answer their questions. Besides, I wanted to kill the locksmith, not myself.

A social worker came in next and began asking the same kinds of questions. "Is anyone hurting you? Are you okay at home? Do you want to go to a women's shelter?" I told her that I was fine and that I had just made a comment in poor taste. I had never had any intent of hurting myself or anyone else. I explained that the secretary for the locksmith company had called the police as a way of getting back at me. After I had answered her questions to her satisfaction, I was left in the exam room for observation for another hour or two. The doctors diagnosed me with stress and released me.

I didn't know if I was I being released to go home or if I was going to be arrested for the comment I had made. As I walked out of the exam room, I didn't see any officers waiting for me. I was a little afraid to leave the hospital, because I was worried that the police would be waiting for me outside. I was a nervous wreck as I slowly made my way to the exit, but I walked out the door. I took a deep breath and waited to see if anyone was going to say anything or stop me. No one seemed to notice, so I breathed a sigh of relief and kept on walking.

Because the ambulance had brought me to the hospital, I didn't know how I was going to get home. I thought about calling a cab, but I lived in the middle of a suburban part of the city, and a cab would have taken at least an hour to get there. There was still some daylight left, and the hospital was only about ten miles away from home. I decided to walk, because I knew this would give me time to think.

I called Martha on the way home to tell her what had happened. She couldn't believe it. She told me that this wouldn't have happened to me if I were white. I told her how humiliated they had made me feel, and all because of some stupid locksmith. And to top it off, I had to pay for poor work and now pay for someone else to change to the locks. As the darkness fell, I began to cry.

When I got home, I took a shower, prayed about what my uncle had asked of me, and then crawled into bed. My journey had now begun.

Chapter Four

DEATH COMES IN THREES

I DON'T REMEMBER being told much about the day of my birth, but I do know that I was born premature, weighing just four pounds and one ounce. I never saw any of my baby pictures, but my uncle told me that I was bald and so small that my parents used a dresser drawer for my bed because they worried I would fall through the slats in my crib. My uncle would always tease me and say that when I would cry, they would just shut the drawer. We lived in the West in a small two bedroom with one bath. I could hear the floors squeak as I played. My mother had an older daughter, and she had a son who also lived with us.

I don't know much about my mother. There wasn't time to get to know her. I have no pictures of her except the one in the obituary, and no real memories of her to hold on to. No hugs, no laughs, and no tender moments. Everyone tells me that we looked alike. I remember as a child having a cousin who called me "Little Mary." I didn't recognize the name, so I never answered him. *Who is he talking to?* I would wonder. "I'm talking to you," he would say. "You look just like your mother. You have her eyes and her smile."

My mother worked in a beauty shop not far from our house. Sometimes she would take me to work with her. I'd play with the other kids who were in the beauty shop until she had finished with her last customer. Sometimes if my mother was busy, the other ladies would try and comb my hair. "I'll do it," my mother would always say. "Sarah doesn't like for anyone to comb her hair." My hair had grown into long ponytails that tangled easily, and if anyone tried to come near me with a comb or brush, I'd scream at the top of my lungs until they left me alone.

My mother was a small and frail woman. She died of ovarian cancer when I was six years old. By the time she died, the illness had reduced her to nothing but skin and bones. I didn't realize what was going on at the funeral. I just remember sitting there and wishing I could go out and play while the service was going on. I didn't understand what everyone was crying about. I didn't realize that I would never see her again.

I don't remember anything about my father except that I didn't like him very much. I heard rumors from family members that he abused my mother. Three weeks after my mother had died, I came home from school one day to find him lying dead on the floor. I went over to shake him, but there was no answer. I didn't understand why he was so still. I didn't know any better, so I figured he was pretending to be asleep and went out to play. Shortly after, my grandmother arrived and asked, "Where's your father?" It told her that he was inside pretending to be asleep. She went in, and the next thing I remember is the police and the ambulance arriving. I was sent next door. I watched as the paramedics brought my father out on the stretcher, with his face covered. I never saw him again, and I don't remember anything about his funeral.

After that, I went to live with my grandmother (who at the time was my only living grandparent). My grandmother lived down the street—close enough to where I could walk to her house. I remember that she had long braids. She was part Cherokee, and her braids reminded me of the pictures and stories of Indians I had read in storybooks. She would bake cookies for me and do all sorts of things that grandmothers do to spoil their grandchildren.

I would stay with her on weekends, and sometimes she would take me to work with her. She worked as a housekeeper and babysat for a doctor who had three daughters. I had fun going to work with her. It allowed me to be a kid for a while. I enjoyed playing with the little girls. But, like everyone else in my life, a few weeks later she disappeared. She died of a heart attack. The death of her daughter-in-law and the sudden death of her son were more than she could handle.

After my parents and my grandmother died, I lived in our house with my older sister. I don't remember moving back there with her. We were close before mom died. She would take me everywhere, and I remember her friends always saying, "Oh, isn't she cute!" I was a skinny little thing, with big brown eyes and long lashes and I was cute as a button. I don't even remember my sister ever saying goodbye or leaving. One day she was there, and then I never saw her again.

My uncle later told me that he was driving to work one morning when he realized that he hadn't seen my sister and me in a few days. *I'll stop and look in on them on my way home,* he thought. After work, he stopped by. He knocked on the door and called my name. I didn't answer, because I was afraid.

"Sarah, are you in there?" he said again. He must have heard me, because he peeked in the window and saw me hiding. "This is your uncle," he said. "Open the door."

"No," I said. "You told me never to open the door when there wasn't anyone home. You are trying to trick me, and I'm not getting a spanking." I went back to watching TV, eating my potato chips and drinking Kool-Aid. I watched, laughing, as my uncle came in through the window. He chased me, and I ran and jumped on the couch. He began to tickle me, and I laughed so hard that tears rolled down my face.

"Why didn't you let me in?"

"I didn't want you to spank me. You always told me not to open the door when no one was home."

"Where is everyone?"

"I don't know."

My uncle looked around. Just about everything was gone except a few small pieces of furniture, my clothes and toys. I still didn't understand that my parents were not coming back, and I had no idea I'd never see my sister again. I couldn't remember how long I had been alone or if my sister had said she was coming back—just that no one was there and I was afraid. My clothes were dirty, and I was hungry. My uncle took me home with him. We all had dinner. I had a bath, went to bed and fell fast asleep.

The next day, my uncle tried to call other family members to see if they had heard from my sister. No one had. In addition to my uncle, my mother had three sisters. I had only met one of the sisters, as the other two had died in a house fire many years ago. My father had a brother who was a teacher at a university. My uncle asked if anyone was willing to open his or her home to me, but no one wanted to take in another mouth to feed. I could hear them talking, and I began to get scared. The others really didn't care what would happen to me. They didn't want to be bothered.

My uncle didn't want to see me go into the foster care system and decided to talk to his wife about taking me in. She had always wanted a little girl, so they decided to give me a home.

Chapter Five

A NEW HOME

MY UNCLE WAS a handsome man. He was married with two sons, aged four and five, whom I'll call Peter and Paul. The boys shared a room in my uncle's three-bedroom home, which allowed me to have my own room.

I was a quiet child and stayed in my room most of the time, out of the way. I didn't want to cause trouble. I tried not to eat too much. My aunt and uncle told me that I could have whatever I wanted—that it was my home now—but I was confused. I still couldn't figure out what was going on. Where were my mother and father? Where was my grandmother? Where was my sister? Where had they gone without me? Even though my sister was several years older than me, she was my best friend. I trusted her. She took care of me and played with me. We laughed together, and she hugged me all the time. So where was she? I hadn't seen them put her in one of those boxes they had put my mother, father and grandmother in and lower her into the ground, so where was she?

After many phone calls, my uncle discovered that my sister had gone away with this guy she had been seeing. He was the father of her son who lived with us. I cried. How could she just leave without me? I wrote her letters, expecting her to come and get me, but I received no response. So I wrote more letters, but they all went unanswered as well. I was shattered. How could she just stop being my sister? How could she not want to talk with me or even make sure I was okay? How could she stop caring just like that? When my letters kept going unanswered, I decided to come up with a plan to find her.

One day, I was playing in the house when I found a roll of silver dollars. I took them and decided to set out to find my sister. Of course, I didn't get very far—the kids in the neighborhood saw me with the money, and I had to share with them to keep them quiet. One of the kids got caught and had to tell his parents where the money came from. They called my aunt and told her I had the money, and of course they sent me home. My aunt waited until my uncle got home, and then they asked me why I had taken the money. I didn't want them to know that I was running away, so I made up a story. They told me that this was my home and that I could have anything I wanted, but I should ask next time. I said okay.

It was getting close to my birthday. I knew that my sister wouldn't forget and that she'd be back to see me. *She'll have a present for me,* I thought. But my birthday came and went, and still there was no sign of her. Soon the holidays were upon us. I wrote her a letter and her sent cards, but still no answer. Not even one phone call. I was devastated. Why didn't she call? Why didn't she care? She had to have received my letters, because none of them were ever returned.

One day, I overheard my aunt and uncle talking and found out that my sister was somewhere in California. One of my aunts knew where my sister was living, and they were actually in contact. That only made me more confused. Why didn't this aunt have my sister call me? Why hadn't my sister checked on me? I still didn't understand what was going on. I was really mad now, and let me tell you, there is nothing worse than a determined six-year-old. The terrible twos had nothing on me. I went back into my aunt and uncle's room and found some money, but this time I decided to hide it until I could come up with a plan to find my sister.

I was enrolled in a new school. The teachers knew about the death of my parents, so they decided to be helpful by taking up a collection to help with my school expenses. That turned out to be a nightmare. The kids were mean. I could hear them whispering, "That's the girl who doesn't have a mommy or daddy." They repeated comments their parents had said, such as the only reason my aunt and uncle kept me around was for the social security and VA checks they were receiving.

How cruel, I thought. I cried at the thought that no one wanted me. *What was wrong with me?* I wondered. It was hard to believe that the only reason someone wanted me was because they were paid to keep me, and at six years of age I really didn't understand what that meant anyway. But I felt ashamed. Later, I learned that the checks my uncle and aunt received were not even enough to cover a pair of shoes for me. (I had a narrow foot, so my shoes had to be bought in specialty stores and were really expensive.)

My aunt and uncle didn't want to see me feeling hurt because of what was going on, so they spoiled me. I got toys, clothes and just about anything I wanted that they could afford. There were not that many girls in the neighborhood to play with, so I stayed in my room and played by myself most of the time. I figured that I wouldn't disturb anyone that way. I still believed that if I got in the way, I'd have to find another home. Most of the time, my uncle and aunt had to check in on me to make sure I was still there.

My aunt enrolled me in Girl Scouts in the hopes of getting me out of the house and involved in some social activity. It lasted for a little while, but I didn't have much interest. My aunt would do just about anything to get a smile out of me, but nothing could make me happy. They tried to take me to a psychiatrist, but I wouldn't talk with him. He would try and analyze me using silly toy games, but all my toys would die, and that would be the end of that. I would sit there during the session and just look at the psychiatrist without saying a word. Afterward, my uncle and aunt would take me back home, and I'd go back to my room.

Finally, the psychiatrist told my aunt and uncle that if I wouldn't talk with him, they were just wasting their money. He felt that maybe I was too young to understand what had happened to me. *What an idiot,* I thought. I wasn't too young to understand that I had been dumped. No, I got the picture: No one wanted me; no one cared. What I didn't understand was *why.* Had everyone left because of something I had done? Wasn't I pretty enough? Did I eat too much? Was I not smart enough? What was wrong with me?

One of the mothers at our church always did my hair and my aunt's hair first thing every Saturday morning. I would sit in the chair and fall asleep, and when I woke up my hair would be done. Washed, conditioned, blow-dried and braided into long beautiful ponytails with a ribbon. When my head nodded, her hands would move with me. When she started doing a press and curl on my hair, she never burned me once.

Peter and Paul were active in basketball and baseball. My uncle was the coach, and they had practice every night. On the weekends, we went to the park as a family, where Peter and Paul would take turns at batting practice. I had to attend every game, because there was no way my aunt and uncle would leave me at home by myself. Besides, I was scared of my own shadow. ("Chicken," my brothers would always call me.)

When I was old enough to be left at home, the minute the car pulled out of the garage, I would run and let our German Shepherd, Snow, in the house. He became my new best friend. He protected me. One morning on the way to the bus stop, one of the neighbors jumped out of the bushes and scared me. I screamed and Snow leaped over the fence, bit him and went back home. In the afternoon when he would hear the school bus, he would jump the fence and run to the bus stop to wait for us. We would play for a while, and then we would put him back in the yard.

I remember getting my brothers in trouble all the time because they were not allowed to hit me. So when I was mad at them, I'd scream and say that they hit me. They would get in trouble, but they would always get me back.

We would always have dinner as a family every night. As we sat at the table, we would have to talk about how we were doing in school, what homework we had, and anything else we needed to tell our parents before someone else did. My aunt was a teacher, and it seemed that she knew everyone. If something happened at school, most of the time she knew it before we got home. If something happened in our neighborhood, she and my uncle were sure to find out. Talk about neighborhood watch! Someone was always looking out the windows where we lived.

We would go out to dinner on Sundays. I always sat in the middle of the back seat, between my brothers. One Sunday, they decided to see if my hair would catch on fire. They pushed in the cigarette lighter, and when it got blazing hot, they stuck one of my ponytails into the lighter to see if it would burn. "What is that smell?" my uncle said. "Is something burning?" I told him it was my hair. Needless to say, my brothers got in a lot of trouble.

We went to church every Sunday. My aunt's father was the minister. Most of the time we spent the whole day in church. When he would preach out of town, Grandpa would always come and get us at five in the morning so he could make it in time to preach his sermon. He loved to fish and always wanted his grandchildren to go along with him. I remember Peter and Paul chasing me with worms and fish. I'd always scream and then go sit in the car and lock the doors. We would catch some fish, clean them and take them home for dinner. Talk about a fish fry.

We lived in a neighborhood where our school was close enough to walk to school every day. We'd play in the evenings. I remember the first time I got my training wheels off my bike, we were racing when I saw a car coming. I panicked, hit the curb, and broke my tooth. I ended up having to have it pulled, which led to my first experience at the dentist's office. It took three nurses to hold me down.

By the time I started junior high, I'd been with my new family for such a long time that no one really talked about my parents anymore. I was still a quiet and shy kid, and I didn't have very many friends. I went through high school feeling invisible. I was a skinny, geeky-looking kid with thick glasses who no one ever really noticed. I wasn't one of the "it" girls—you know, one of the really pretty and cool girls—so I didn't see any reason to go to any of the parties. I went on my first date to the junior prom, but it didn't go very well. We came home right afterward and skipped all of the after parties. During my senior year, a group of girls went to the prom together, and I was invited to join them. It was fun.

Sounds like a normal life, right? It was on the outside, but not on the inside. I was normal to the naked eye, but on the inside I was broken. I always expected people to die or leave. Because of the abandonment I had experienced as a child, I grew up thinking that it was normal to just walk out of relationships or situations I didn't like. I was always prepared to move on, and I always kept people at a distance, never allowing them to form relationships with me. The pain I endured as a child grew with me as I grew up. It became rooted inside and affected everything I did.

Chapter Six

MAKING THE CALL

MY TRIALS CAME at such an early age that I didn't really understand what was going on. As a result, I erased it from my mind, pretending it never happened, and allowed my bitterness to turn within. Wrong thought patterns started developing that I would carry into my adult life. I felt rejected as a child, and as a result I grew angry. I was withdrawn. I developed low self-esteem and felt inadequate. From my experiences of abandonment, I learned that it was okay to just walk away—that this was how problems were solved. In a sense, my life took on the characteristics my sister demonstrated to me at an early age.

What I didn't realize at the time—even though it was right in front of me—was that I had a lot of positives in my life. I focused on the fact that I had been abandoned, but I had a new home. I focused on the fact that my parents had died and my had sister left, but I had a new family. I focused on the fact that my sister didn't love me, but I had a new family who loved me and was willing to give me anything I needed or wanted. I didn't pay attention to my new family, who were committed to me and each other and never walked away.

Without understanding and the strength to address life's issues, we have a tendency to bury or hide our pain. We gain the wisdom and understanding to address life's issues through the *Word of God*. For me, that was a quiet, internal struggle. Fear was my focus, not the fact that I was safe, had food and clothes and had a great home.

Our family wasn't one of those that said "I love you" often. It was a given. My aunt was a woman of God and had a heart filled with compassion. She took in anyone who needed help. Sometimes I thought she was crazy.

One morning, I woke up and couldn't get in my bathroom. I heard my aunt in the kitchen, so I went in to ask who was in my bathroom. She told me it was a lady she had picked up at the bus station. The lady knew one of our relatives and needed help, so my aunt had gone and picked her up. She was busy cooking breakfast for her.

If someone died, my aunt would bake a cake. If someone needed something, she would give what she could. She was just like a mom to me, so when I got the call saying the doctors had found a lump in her breast, I got in my car and drove home. It was a twelve-hour drive, but I drove straight through, only stopping for gas.

We went to the hospital for the biopsy. Our family waited quietly in the waiting room, watching the clock. Hours passed. Finally, the doctor came out and said that the tumor was non-malignant. We all breathed a sigh of relief. We sat with her for a while, and then we went home. After a few days, my aunt was released from the hospital. We went home and got her settled. I cooked a few meals and put them in the freezer. The next morning, I made the long drive home.

A few years later, my uncle was diagnosed with prostate cancer and was scheduled to have surgery. I was flying home to be with him, but when I got to the airport, the flight was late. I began to panic. I had to be at the hospital before they took my uncle into surgery. I needed him to know that I was there. As I boarded the plane, I told the pilot my situation and asked how late he thought we would be. The pilot said he understood and that he would be able to make up the time once we were in the air. He was right, and as I got off the plane, I thanked him for getting me there on time. "I wish your uncle luck with his surgery," he said.

My cousin picked me up at the airport, and we went straight to the hospital. My uncle was happy to see me, and I was so glad I got there before they gave him the anesthesia. Even though I had never told him, I loved him with all my heart, and I know he loved me.

As with most men, he was cool on the outside, not allowing the worry to show on his face. As we stood in the post-op room, I again thought about what he had said to me many years before: "Before I die, I want you and your sister to get together." We said our goodbyes, and they pushed his hospital bed down the hall. I stood there watching until they wheeled him out of sight.

As I sat in the waiting room, I continued to think about how much he had done for me. He gave me a home when I didn't have one. I always had clothes and enough to eat. I had toys, cars and had gone to school. He had never asked anything of me except for this one thing—that one day I reach out to my sister. I finally decided it was time.

The treatment for the prostate cancer went well, and sometime after my uncle had fully recuperated, I asked him for my sister's number. He didn't comment; he just gave me the number. I dialed it, and a child answered.

"Hello," I said. "Is Eve there?"

"Yes," the voice answered. "Who's calling?"

"Her sister," I replied. I hadn't acknowledged her as my sister in years. My heart pounded as I heard footsteps coming to the phone.

"Hello," a voice said. "This is Eve." I was shocked that she had actually answered the phone. After all, she had avoided me for all these years.

"Hi," I said. "This is Sarah. How are you?" I didn't really know what to say after that. It was a difficult conversation. She wanted to know all about me and asked me all kinds of questions: Was I married? Did I have a family? She even tried to give me sisterly advice at one point, and it took everything in me not to lose it. She had some nerve to act like she still had the right to give me advice! But I didn't say anything. This was the moment I had been waiting for, to give her a piece of my mind, to call her a thing or two. I wanted to do anything I could to hurt her the way she had hurt me. But I didn't say anything.

My sister asked if I went to church and if I had a relationship with God. Finally, neutral ground. This was something we could talk about. As we talked, I realized that I had to let go of the right I thought I had to punish her. I had desperately wanted to hurt her for so many years, but in that moment I understood that I had to just let it go. I knew that the hatred I felt for her was keeping me from a true and meaningful relationship with God.

Eve said she was going to be in Las Vegas and wanted to know if I would come down to see her. I heard myself say, "Yes, I will meet you," while at the same time wondering who this person was on the phone who was agreeing to do this. I know it definitely wasn't me.

The next morning, my friend Ruth came to my office. I hadn't seen her in a long time. Most of the time, Ruth and I passed each other in the hall, exchanging greetings and quick conversations before we ran back off to our offices and our busy schedules. But this particular morning, Ruth came to my office and asked how I was doing. She said that the Holy Spirit had led her to me and told her that she had to physically come by my office today. She wasn't sure why.

"How are you doing?" she asked. I responded in the usual manner, telling her about all the work and home stuff I had going on at the time.

"No, that's not it," she replied. So I shared other filler stuff that was going on.

"No," she again replied. "That's not it." I finally decided to tell her about the decision I had made to forgive my sister.

"Okay," she said. "Now I know why I am here."

God uses people with similar experiences to speak into our lives and help us through our trials. That's why Ruth was there—she had been led by the Holy Spirit to help me. As we talked, she shared her ordeal with me. My heart bled. I was shocked. Here before me was a beautiful woman, 5'11", 145 pounds, with long black hair. I couldn't believe what she was telling me. Yet there she stood in front of me, willing to open old wounds in order to help me. We talked about how she had been adopted and about her new family. We talked about the heartache and longing she had felt to find her real parents—and her fear of what would happen if she did.

I shared with her a dream I had been having. I would see myself swimming in a large body of water, and there on the shore, Jesus would be waiting. He was there cheering me on. Then I suddenly went under, but Jesus kept calling me and cheering me on. He would say, "I have prayed for you. I know you can do it." As I tried to swim to him, my heart would get heavy. I could see myself getting tired and start to drown. I was fighting to stay afloat, but I could hear Jesus say, "Let go. Don't hold on to the hatred; surrender it to me."

After making several attempts, I finally let go (I really had no choice—I was exhausted) and made it to shore. I could see Jesus hugging me and telling me how much He loved me and how happy He was that I had made the decision to let go of the bondage that had been weighing me down. As we sat on the shore looking out at the water, He reminded me of Peter walking on the water and how when Peter got afraid he began to drown. He held my hand and told me that He would always be there and would never leave me. I had made it through the toughest part of my journey, which was the decision to follow Him. He knew that I would make mistakes, but He said that as long as I got up and kept on trying, He would always be there waiting to help me. Even when it didn't feel like He was there.

Chapter Seven

THE VISIT

I KNEW THAT forgiving my sister for abandoning me as a child would be hard, to put it mildly. My sister had hurt me so much that I could not even say her name. I still couldn't believe she had just cut me off like that, without a word. I knew it would take a miracle for me to do this, so I started praying for one.

I remembered that a friend had given me a book on fasting. I found it and began to browse through it. One Scripture in particular caught my attention: "Is not this the kind of *fasting* I have chosen: to loose the chains of injustice and untie the cords of the yoke, to set the oppressed free and break every yoke?" (Isaiah 58:6 Italics added). This was exactly what I wanted to accomplish: to break the chain of unforgiveness and set my heart free.

In my mind, I couldn't imagine how I was going to be able to let go, but I knew that in Philippians 4:13 Paul had said, "I can do all things through Him who gives me strength." I also knew that I had to believe I could forgive my sister and even face her one day. Then another passage caught my eye: In Matthew 17:20-21, Jesus said to His disciples, "Assuredly, I say to you, if you have faith as a mustard seed, you will say to this mountain, 'Move from here to there,' and it will move; and nothing will be impossible for you. However, this kind does not go out except by *prayer and fasting*" (Italics added). I realized that my lack of faith could keep me from accomplishing what I had set out to do. It's a bit like the Little Engine who thought he could.

As I continued to pray, it became clear to me that fasting: the setting aside a special time to seek God on the matter was the right thing to do. I decided to enter into a forty-day fast, because of its significance in the Bible. Jesus was in the wilderness for forty days; Moses was on Mount Sinai with the Lord receiving instruction (The Ten Commandments) for forty days and nights; it rained for forty days and nights. Forty days to a breakthrough seemed logical. I prayed that God would give me the strength to get through it.

I wanted God to understand that I was serious in my desire to break the hardness in my heart and the bitterness I felt toward my sister, so I decided to also offer a sacrifice. I wanted to sacrifice what my flesh craved the most, and one of my biggest temptations was sugar. I was such a junk food eater, that some evenings would come home and just have a bag of gummy bears for dinner. So I decided to give up sugar and snacking during my fast. I limited myself to fish, fruit and vegetables—no cake, chocolate, ice cream or candy. I really loved sugar, so I also prayed that God would give me strength to let go of my addiction. I told myself that if Jesus would not come down from the cross just to save Himself for an imperfect person like me, then I could give up sugar for forty days and stop getting up in the middle of the night for refrigerator raids.

I began my fast with a determined spirit. My mind was made up: *I was going to do this.* That was half the battle. A week before I actually began the fast, I began to prepare myself by praying, "Jesus, if You can stay on the cross and do what You did for me so that I a sinner like me might be saved, then I can complete this fast and let this bitterness I am holding against my sister go. I will be able to meet her with a loving heart." I wanted to actually be able to say what I hadn't said in years: that I had a sister. I had always said that my mother had another daughter, but I never called her my sister. So I prayed this prayer every day and had communion, the partaking of the body (bread) and the blood (wine or in this case grape juice) of Christ in remembrance of what God had done. Then I began studying all the scriptures I could find on forgiveness, noting what they taught about forgiveness and the examples they gave.

Each day, I read my Bible and prayed. I prayed the Lord's Prayer and concentrated on the portion that said, "Forgive us our sins, as we also forgive everyone who sins against us" (Luke 11:4). I prayed and cried until I could feel the stronghold that Satan had on me being released. I let go and allowed God do a work in me. I could feel the pain slowly leaving my body. I realized that I wasn't just forgiving my sister for my uncle; I was doing it for *me*.

God had taken my hand and led me along on this journey. He had brought that which I had hidden in the darkness of my soul to light and had begun to purge me of the bitterness, wrong attitudes and other characteristics that were not of Him. He was cleansing me and healing me so that I could later be used to help someone else. As I worked my way through my fast, I began to see flickers of light. The more I yielded, the closer I got to the light. Whenever I fought against His will, the darkness would again begin to cover me. To me, this was a sign God was using to direct me on my path. If I followed Him I'd see the light, but if I stepped off the path, I would be covered in darkness. Needless to say, I was afraid of the dark, and whenever I strayed from the path I would hurry to find my way back to the light.

For the first time, I found that I could say my sister's name. She was no longer my mother's other daughter. As I continued my fast, I was surprised to find that I not only prayed for myself but also for my sister. I prayed that God would take away the guilt she must have been feeling for leaving me and that she would be able to forgive herself. It must have been difficult for her to make that kind of a decision and never look back. I can only imagine the guilt and torment she must have gone through. My preparation time was coming to an end and I could feel my heart changing, but my journey was not over. I still had to face her. I knew it would take a lot to show kindness and restrain myself from lashing out when we met, but I made the choice that nothing would stop me from the promise I had made to God.

We had arranged to meet in Las Vegas at the end of the forty days at my uncle's house. The night before I was supposed to get on the road and drive home to meet her, I began to feel sick. *I can't get sick now,* I thought. I decided to go anyway. No matter what, I would not miss this trip. I would not miss the opportunity to see Eve after all these years.

That morning I woke up in a sweat and was filled with chills, but I packed my bags and loaded the car. I prayed, because I knew that this was Satan trying to make me miss my blessing. Whatever happened, I wouldn't turn back now. I held my head as I pulled out of the driveway at 4 A.M. It was at least 90 degrees outside, but by the time I got to the outskirts of

Los Angeles, the chills were getting worse. I pulled off to stop at a store to buy a jacket. The lady thought I was crazy. Here it was the middle of summer, and I was looking for a jacket. I called my friends from the highway, and they urged me to turn around. I told them no. No matter what, I was going through with it.

Right before I crossed the Nevada State line, I rear-ended a truck. I wasn't hurt and there was little damage to his truck, but my car was a different story. The front wheel well was mangled. Satan was trying to stop me from reaching my destination, but I was determined to continue. I drove until I was about 100 miles outside of Las Vegas and then pulled over and called my cousin. He came and got me, and I slept at his house that night. The next day, still weak, I pressed on. I made it to my uncle's house, only to pull into the driveway and have the tire fall apart. Unknown to me, as I drove the car and the wheel turned, the tread was being cut from the tire. For the last six hours of my drive, God kept that tire together, allowing me to make it home safely.

That afternoon we took the car to a shop, where a mechanic fixed the wheel well and changed the tire. I came back home to see if my uncle had heard from Eve, but he hadn't. My temperature got worse, so I went to lie down. A little later, I went to the hospital, where the doctors gave me a strong dose of antibiotics.

When I got back home, there was still no word from my sister. My uncle was worried, so he called Eve. I could hear him talking, and then yelling from my room. She was still in California. I had never heard my uncle so angry. "Why didn't you let her know you weren't coming to meet her?" he yelled. "She drove for twelve hours, sick, and you stood her up!" *She did it again*, I thought. It was the same thing she had done all my life. I really thought that this time she would show up, but she didn't.

It was a long twelve-hour ride home, but I made the choice that her not showing up wasn't going to bother me this time. After I returned home, I continued to reach out to her but, as usual, she didn't respond. I sent her pictures, but never got any in return. That day, I buried the need for her to love me. After thirty-seven years, the chain of bitterness had been broken. I had gone through so much sadness and wasted so much time seeking her affection. I realized that I would never get that back, but now it was time to press forward and stop living in the past. It was time to start looking to the future.

Chapter Eight

TRAGEDY STRIKES AGAIN

CHECKING MY PHONE messages one day, I listened to one from my aunt telling me that Miriam, my sister's youngest daughter, had called to say that Eve was sick and in the hospital. My aunt gave me the phone number that she'd left and the name of the hospital that Eve was in. I called Miriam told her who I was, and asked what was going on. She said that during the past year, my sister had been diagnosed with cancer and that they had taken her to the hospital. She was in intensive care, and her organs were failing. They didn't expect her to make it through the night, but she was still hanging on.

Three years had passed since we talked, but without hesitation, I called the airline and booked a flight to leave the next day. I had no idea what I'd say to her. I wanted to ask why she didn't keep in touch with me. Family is family, and even if she couldn't take care of me, why didn't she keep in touch? But more than that, I wanted to let her know that I forgave her. No matter what the reason was for what she did, I forgave her. I didn't want her to have that on her mind in her last days.

I went to work and let them know that I would be out for a couple of days. I made arrangements for my dog to stay at the sitter's and went home to pack my things. Before I could leave for the airport, I got a call that Eve had died. I didn't know what to feel. I prayed and asked God why He hadn't allowed me to see her and talk with her. God whispered, "It's not about you." I knew that He was in control and that it wasn't meant for me to see her. I asked that God would give her peace.

I decided to wait until Eve's funeral service was scheduled to fly out to Las Vegas. I spoke with Miriam every day. It was strange talking with her. She was my niece, but we had never talked before. My sister had six kids, and I didn't know any of them. They were my nieces and nephews, and I didn't even know their names.

The funeral was scheduled for the following Tuesday. I made reservations for my aunt, uncle and myself. Both of them had siblings in Los Angeles. My aunt had the opportunity to see her brother several times a year because they travelled back and forth from Vegas to Los Angeles, but my uncle hadn't seen his sister in years. He was now seventy-seven, so I thought this would be a great opportunity for him to see his family.

Shortly after, I got a call from Miriam telling me the funeral had been pushed back a week. I asked what was going on, and she said that they didn't realize that their mother's insurance policy had lapsed and that the insurance company was not going to pay for the burial. Meanwhile, as they were trying to get things straightened out with the insurance company, Eve's body was being moved around.

Even though my sister had walked out on me and hurt me beyond belief, I agreed to pick up to the remaining cost for the funeral. No matter what she had done to me, I couldn't imagine going through the pain of cancer and then not being able to be laid to rest. Miriam shared with me that Eve had to have steel pins placed in her hip because her bones had deteriorated. I could tell that she loved her mother. She had been the one responsible for staying with her and talking care of her. Her illness required someone to be with her twenty-four hours a day.

I kept postponing my flight. First I was to leave on Friday, then on Saturday, then on Sunday, and then finally I flew out on Monday morning. I didn't know how I was going to feel or how I would react to seeing my sister's body.

When my flight landed, I grabbed my luggage, picked up the rental car and called Ester, a young lady who had helped so much at the mortuary. I found out the mortuary wasn't far from the airport, so I went right over. When I got there, Ester and I talked for a while and went over the cost of the funeral. She gave me the picture that she had in the file of Eve. I looked at it, but I didn't feel anything. I couldn't even tell if it was my sister. After a while, Miriam showed up at the mortuary. I asked Ester to have her wait outside for a minute so I could prepare myself. I told her that I hadn't met Eve's family before. Miriam came in, and we shook hands. We talked about the funeral arrangements and kept things business-like.

I left the mortuary and went to my aunt Rachael's house, where I relaxed until my cousin got off work. My cousin was a year older than me and had always been a good listener. When she got off work, I went over to her house to spend the night. When I got there, we talked about what was going on. She thought I was crazy to offer to pay for the funeral. I thought so too, but I had made a commitment to be a living example of what love, kindness and compassion meant. I wanted to be an example of putting the past behind and doing what was right—whether my sister deserved it or not.

The next day, I went and picked up my aunt and uncle and took them to see my aunt Rebecca. While we were visiting and talking about old times, Ester called and said the body was ready for viewing, so we went by to look at it. I was uncomfortable, to say the least, and glad that my aunt and uncle were with me. My uncle recognized my sister right away. I still didn't know what to think. I still didn't feel anything. I didn't know her. I wasn't even sure that this was my sister I was looking at. Like my mother, the cancer had taken a toll on her body, and she was small and frail. I couldn't help but think, *After all this time, I didn't feel anything, not even anger.*

After we left the mortuary, we had lunch and went shopping. The day was warm and beautiful, so my aunt and uncle and I went for a walk. Afterward, we went back to my aunt's brother's house and relaxed. Later that afternoon, we called Miriam to let her know that my uncle wanted to see all of Eve's kids. We set up a meeting with them, and that evening we drove over to their house. It was strange. My uncle recognized some of Eve's children, but a few of them he didn't recognize at all.

They had a nice home, nice cars and didn't seem to be wanting for anything, which made me feel worse because my uncle had always told me that maybe Eve didn't have much and couldn't afford to take care of me. He had always told me that she'd had a hard life, but all the Mercedes outside didn't fit his story. So now that theory was blown out the window. That was when they showed me the funeral program. They had put my name down to provide a tribute for a loving sister. That was about all I could take. I hit the roof. I was angry. A tribute! Remarks maybe, but a *tribute*! A tribute to a woman who had treated me so cruelly! At that moment,

I regretted paying for the funeral. What was I thinking? I didn't think I could stay there any longer. I gave my uncle that "you better get me out of here" look and went into the kitchen. We talked for a minute, and I told him I couldn't take it anymore and wanted to go home. So we left.

It was a quiet ride home. No one said a word. When we finally arrived home, I went straight to bed and cried in my pillow. I prayed and asked God to direct me as to what I was supposed to say. Should I even show up at the funeral? *That's it,* I thought, *I won't show up.* That would solve everything. I would fly back early. But what would my aunt and uncle think? I wanted them to be able to stay at the funeral as long as they wanted, so I decided to hire a limousine to drive them around that day. I only had three days off and would have to leave. I needed to get back to work. Actually, I *wanted* to get back to work.

At about 4 A.M., the Holy Spirit woke me and told to me what He wanted me to say. He wanted me to talk about unconditional love and sacrifice! I got up, picked up some paper from the fax machine and began to write down everything that came to me. I wrote and cried and wrote and cried. Then I went back to sleep for about an hour.

I woke up, got dressed and ate breakfast. I was calm, but as soon as I started driving to the funeral service, the fear hit me. I was frantically calling my prayer partners one after the other, trying to reach someone to pray with me. I needed someone to help me get through this funeral. Finally, I reached my friend Ruth and told her that I couldn't go through with it. She reminded me that it was only Satan. I knew she was right, but could I fight him off this time? This was the hurt of all hurts in my life, and I didn't know if I was I strong enough to face it. *When I am weak, He is my strength,* I reminded myself. *Greater is He who is in me than he that is in the world.* I quoted scripture after scripture, but my heart still pounded.

When I arrived at the church, I saw that the family was lining up. I closed my eyes, and my friend prayed over me. When I opened my eyes, I noticed that they had all gone inside the church, so I told Ruth that I had to go in. I took a deep breath and searched for peace. I thought about Peter walking on water and how he had begun to sink when he was afraid. I resolved not to let this situation steal my peace, so I searched for a still place—a place where I could be still for a minute and let God take control. I needed God to comfort me and help me though this.

I walked into the church and sat down in the third row next to my aunt and uncle. I was invited to sit on the front row with my sister's children, but I wanted to stay where I knew I was safe. I stared out the window and noticed how scenic the view was. The trees, the sky and the mountains were beautiful, and the sky was so clear that I could see for miles. This was the day the Lord had made, and what a glorious day it was. *It's picture perfect*, I thought.

As I sat there listening to the remarks being made about my sister, it was like a nightmare coming to life. I was tormented. I was hurt. Everyone talked about what a wonderful person my sister was. How she loved everyone and took them into her home. How she would feed the kids in the neighborhood. My view of her wasn't loving at all. I sat there thinking, *What a bunch of lies. She tossed me, her own sister, aside like yesterday's leftover trash. She didn't love everyone—or was it just me she couldn't stand?* I remember so many times as a child thinking, *If only I were prettier...if only I didn't eat so much...if only I were smarter, then she would want me.* Then I heard a whisper: *But I love you just the way you are.*

I fought back the tears as I continued to stare out the window. I realized that my sister had not only broken my heart but also shattered it into pieces. Her rejection had changed the way I thought of myself and others. The day she walked away—without looking back once—had left me feeling like I wasn't worthy of anyone's love. That was why I had never been able to truly give or receive love. I didn't know how. I was too afraid to trust anyone with my heart again.

As an innocent child, I had adored my sister and looked up to her. We were so close before our mother died. How could that just change over night? The love of a sister was supposed to be special, but Eve had destroyed what I thought family was all about. I guess that's why I had settled for relationships where I wasn't happy. I just wanted to be loved, even if I didn't love the person back. I wanted to think that I was worthy of love and that I would be happy just because someone finally loved me. I thought in some way that would validate the fact that my sister was wrong—that I *was* lovable. At that moment, I heard a whisper again: *But I love you.*

Soon it was time for me to go up to the podium to make my remarks. Satan was busy as the spiritual warfare raged inside of me. I could literally see a picture of a devil on one shoulder and an angel on the other. I could hear the devil saying "tell them what you really think about her. This is your last chance." It would have been so easy for me to turn that funeral into total disaster. The angel kept saying show her love little one, isn't that what I've done for you? I kept thinking what the Word of God tells us, that greater is He who is in me than he who is in the world. Eve may have been my blood, but Jesus gave His blood for me. And because of what God did for me, I chose to place a guard over my tongue.

I had to choose to extend love where it wasn't deserved, just as Jesus extended His love for me every day. The Word tells us that there is no blessing in loving those who love us; that the greater blessing is in loving our enemy or in loving those who have hurt us (see Matthew 5:44-46). After all, Eve had told me that she had found Christ, and I'm a living witness that God changes people.

Chapter Nine

STRENGTH BEYOND MEASURE

I LOOKED OUT at the audience, smiled and said, "Good morning, church." I got a weak response, so I said "good morning" again with passion. "What a beautiful day for a homecoming. When I heard that Eve was in the hospital and that her organs were failing, I booked a flight for the next day. I wanted to get here because there was so much to say, so much to talk about. But she died before I could get on my flight. I asked God why He had taken her before I got a chance to talk to her." *Before I got a chance to say goodbye and tell her that I forgave her for the past,* I thought to myself. I wanted her to be at peace and not die with any guilt over leaving me or for not keeping in touch.

"Her family said that she was in pain," I continued, "so I thought I would also read the Bible to her. But God said, 'Sarah, it's not about you.' As I prayed about what to say here today, I asked the Holy Spirit to speak to me—to let my words be about what God wanted and not of me. For my words were for those who lived, and I knew God would want me to be an extension of His love and kindness. And as I prayed, I began to cry.

"I thought about one of my favorite songs, 'Great is Your Mercy,' and great indeed was God's mercy toward me. And as I told the Lord that I couldn't do this, He said, 'You can do all things though Christ who strengthens you. I am with you.' I thought about the cross and the sacrifice the Lord had made for me. *That unconditional love of God—that's what family was all about,* I said to myself. Love and sacrifice. That's what Eve had shown to her family, and that's what my aunt and uncle who raised me had shown me. That's what God did for all of us the day He died on Calvary."

I turned and looked at the huge cross to the side of me and said, "LOVE and SACRIFICE." I went on to say that I had asked a friend what she thought unconditional love meant, and she had said, "Extending love and kindness when it is not deserved." Again, I thought about the cross. Each turn I made and each thought I had led me to the cross and to God's unconditional love for me—the love and sacrifice He made for me.

"I didn't have much time with Eve," I went on to say, "but the last time we talked, we talked about the Lord. I was glad to know that she knew my heavenly Father. So now, there is no more sickness and no more pain. When He comes again, when He calls us up, we will be reunited in heaven, Eve and I. There, we will walk around heaven all day. But until then, my sister, may you rest."

I went to the ladies' room after I had finished my remarks to compose myself. I stood there in front of the mirror, again thinking about God's unconditional love. For it was that love that had got me through this difficult situation. It was that love that had given me the strength I needed when I needed it the most.

Just then a lady walked in. She came over to me and said, "You look just like you did as a child." I didn't recognize her, so her comments left me a bit confused.

"I'm sorry," I said. "Do I know you?"

"I worked with your sister, and I know what happened," she said. "She was so proud of you. You were all she talked about. She said she really loved you, but she never got a chance to tell you."

I was shocked. I didn't know what else to say but "really?" All the while, I was thinking, *But my sister didn't know anything about me.*

I returned to my seat and sat down. I turned back to the window and thought about what a sister really was to me. That day, I realized that a sister was my cousin and my friends who had always made time to listen to me and been there for me through the good and the bad. Sure, we had our days, but the love was unconditional. I knew I could count on any one of them. "Sisters" were the ladies whom God had used to speak into my life in their own unique way; sisters in Christ that God used to help me in my journey.

I left immediately after the service and changed clothes at aunt Rachel's house. She said that she was proud of me and that my words had blessed her. She commented as to how strong I was and said that she would not have been able to do it. We talked about the Lord and how I felt that this was what God would have me to do—to show kindness. I told her that the comments I made were not of me. My words were not for the dead, but for the living. I told her that God was too good for me to do anything else other than show kindness. After all, what purpose would it serve? Kindness and love were greater.

As I later drove to the airport, the war continued inside of me. Satan kept telling me, "Your own family didn't love you." But God was doing a new thing, and again I turned my thoughts to the cross and to God's grace. I told myself, *God never walked out. He is and was always there, just waiting on me.*

As I sat in the airport, tears streamed down my face. In my head I could still hear everyone talking about how my sister loved everyone. I had to keep telling myself that God loved me, and that was more than enough. A lady next to me asked, "Are you okay?" "Yes," I replied, "I just left a funeral."

A funeral indeed. It was time to bury the past. It was time to let it go. I boarded the plane and fell asleep. My flight landed safely, and I cried as I drove home.

THE FAST
A FORTY-DAY JOURNEY

IN THIS NEXT section of this book, you will dive deeper into the Word of God. It is my prayer that as you read and study these pages, you will learn how to apply the Word of God to your specific situation and experience the same freedom I had in overcoming unforgiveness.

In chapter one, we talked about making choices and the three things required to make a change: (1) having a *desire* to change, (2) having *faith* that you will change, and (3) refocusing your thoughts.

On Days 1-14 of our journey, we will study several instances in the Word of God where we are called to forgive. These were the scriptures that created the *desire* in me to forgive. In corporate America, I guess you would call this the "business case," or in a court of law, the "compelling argument."

On Days 15-22, we will next look at examples of people in the Bible who forgave their enemies and overcame offenses. These scriptures demonstrated *faith* to me and made me believe that I could forgive.

On Days 23-30, we will look at God's healing power. As I studied these pages, I realized that the word "heal" has many different meanings. Jesus was not only concerned with physical healing but also the healing of minds and spirits of those who suffered. God is no respecter of persons, so if He could do it for the people in the Bible and me, He is able to do the same for you. Note how He brought the characters in the Bible through their trials.

On Days 31-38, we will begin the *task of renewing our minds by* looking at what God says about us. This was also an important part of my healing process. Renewing my mind meant changing how I thought. It was a reprogramming my thoughts, so to speak.

I wanted to know more about who I was. Instead I found out WHOSE I was. Now, most people would start with their family tree, but for me to understand my roots, I needed to know more about God, my creator. I wanted to develop a deeper relationship with Him.

Additionally, after forgiving my sister and beginning the process of letting go of the abandonment, I thought everything would fall into place. But I still wasn't experiencing the peace and joy I thought I would. There was still something missing. My heart was free of the bitterness, but I still didn't feel that deep-down joy. I realized that I was still being haunted by the negative voices I referred to at the beginning of this book—the ones that filled me with doubt and fear. These negative voices were a constant reminder of my past and every mistake I had made. They kept me filled with seeds of negativity. I found that these scriptures filled me with confidence, worth and self-esteem.

On Day 39, we will study what love really is, for without it we have nothing. And on Day 40, we will close out our journey with a few final instructions—instructions that I pray you will heed.

Review the scriptures and exercises daily. I suggest you start a journal of forgiveness. As you work through your forty-day fast, capture the forgiveness that God extends to you and begin to extend that forgiveness to others. You may take more than one journey to forgiveness and healing. Do not skip ahead, but take your time and really focus on developing your relationship with God. Remember, God is no respecter of persons. If He could heal my heart and help me to forgive my sister, He will give you the strength to forgive the people in your life. You are accountable for your actions to God, so even if someone doesn't forgive you, you have to release him or her.

Setting Up Your Fast

To help you with your fast, here are a few things you should think about before you get started.

Determine what your goal will be for the fast. I fasted for deliverance from unforgiveness and hardness of heart. Pray and ask God to lead you in your decision.

Establish a certain time of the day in which you will spend time with God. I prayed and meditated first thing in the morning. I found that when I did, God spoke to me throughout the day. Be consistent in your daily devotion to God.

Determine if you will offer a sacrifice and what that sacrifice will be. I gave up sugar. Think about what's important and/or right for you. Will you give up one meal a day, or one a week? If you are making a drastic change in your eating routine, consult your physician. (Especially if you are on medication, as you will need to make sure that fasting is safe for you). Some have given up TV and sat quietly and read the Word or spent an hour or two doing volunteer work each week. Decide what's right for you and stick to it.

DAY ONE

Forgiving Others

Scripture for the Day

> Forgive us our debts as we forgive our debtors...For if you forgive men when they sin against you, your heavenly father will forgive you. But if you do not forgive men their sins, your father will not forgive your sins.
>
> —Matthew 6:12,14-15

> Be kind and compassionate to one another, forgiving each other, just as in Christ God forgave you.
>
> —Ephesians 4:32

These were critical scriptures for me, which is why I lead off the fast with them. As I read them, I thought about all the things I've done wrong in my life and how many times I had asked God to forgive me. I wanted God to forgive my sins, so I knew I had to forgive others. So, when you think about it, how can you *not* forgive someone? Don't you want to be forgiven?

Study for the Day

Read Mathew 6. Ask God to reveal any unforgiveness in your heart so that you may be in line with His Word and so that you may forgive and be forgiven. Is there anyone with whom you need to reconcile? If you can, go to that person. If not, repent and release it to God.

_____

_____

_____

_____

_____

_____

_____

Day Two

Self-Righteousness

Scripture for the Day

But Jesus went to the Mount of Olives.

At dawn he appeared again in the temple courts, where all the people gathered around him, and he sat down to teach them. The teachers of the law and the Pharisees brought in a woman caught in adultery. They made her stand before the group and said to Jesus, "Teacher, this woman was caught in the act of adultery. In the Law Moses commanded us to stone such women. Now what do you say?" They were using this question as a trap, in order to have a basis for accusing him.

But Jesus bent down and started to write on the ground with his finger. When they kept on questioning him, he straightened up and said to them, "If any one of you is without sin, let him be the first to throw a stone at her." Again he stooped down and wrote on the ground.

At this, those who heard began to go away one at a time, the older ones first, until only Jesus was left, with the woman still standing there. Jesus straightened up and asked her, "Woman, where are they? Has no one condemned you?"

"No one, sir," she said.

"Then neither do I condemn you," Jesus declared. "Go now and leave your life of sin."

—John 8:1-11

Study for the Day

None of us is perfect, for we all fall short of the glory of God. I found myself asking God to forgive me of my self-righteousness. We all have a tendency to think that we are right all the time. I have learned to ask God to convict my heart about situations. God is always fair and just.

Make a list of all the people you are casting stones at. Now take that list and write down the things you have done to others that might cause them to want to throw stones at you. Pray over the list and ask God to convict your heart over the matter. Where you owe a person an apology, extend one, if you can. Regardless, let go of all of it and move on.

_____

_____

_____

_____

_____

_____

_____

_____

_____

_____

_____

_____

_____

_____

_____

_____

_____

_____

_____

_____

_____

_____

_____

_____

DAY THREE

The Parable of the Unmerciful Servant

Scripture for the Day

Then Peter came to Jesus and asked, "Lord, how many times shall I forgive my brother when he sins against me? Up to seven times?"

Jesus answered, "I tell you, not seven times, but seventy-seven times.

"Therefore, the kingdom of heaven is like a king who wanted to settle accounts with his servants. As he began the settlement, a man who owed him ten thousand talents was brought to him. Since he was not able to pay, the master ordered that he and his wife and his children and all that he had be sold to repay the debt.

"The servant fell on his knees before him. 'Be patient with me,' he begged, 'and I will pay back everything.' The servant's master took pity on him, cancelled the debt and let him go.

"But when that servant went out, he found one of his fellow servants who owed him a hundred denarii. He grabbed him and began to choke him. 'Pay back what you owe me!' he demanded.

"His fellow servant fell to his knees and begged him, 'Be patient with me, and I will pay you back.'

"But he refused. Instead, he went off and had the man thrown into prison until he could pay the debt. When the other servants saw what had happened, they were greatly distressed and went and told their master everything that had happened.

"Then the master called the servant in. 'You wicked servant,' he said, 'I cancelled all that debt of yours because you begged me to. Shouldn't you have had mercy on your fellow servant just as I had on you?' In anger his master turned him over to the jailers to be tortured, until he should pay back all he owed.

"This is how my heavenly Father will treat each of you unless you forgive your brother from your heart."

—Matthew 18:21-35

Study for the Day

God has forgiven you countless times, and there is no end to His grace and mercy. Do not keep count or play offenses over and over again in your mind. That will only keep you focused on the issue, and the more you focus on it, the more it will keep your heart hardened (or, like me, it will keep your heart in knots). What offenses are you focusing on? List them, pray about them, and then release them to the Lord.

_____

_____

_____

_____

_____

_____

_____

_____

_____

_____

_____

_____

_____

_____

_____

_____

_____

_____

_____

DAY FOUR

Judging Others

Scripture for the Day

Do not judge, and you will not be judged. Do not condemn, and you will not be condemned. Forgive, and you will be forgiven. Give and it will be given to you.

—Luke 6:37

Do not judge, or you too will be judged. For in the same way you judge others, you will be judged, and with the measure you use, it will be measured to you.

—Matthew 7:1-2

You judge by human standards; I pass judgment on no one. But if I do judge, my decisions are right, because I am not alone. I stand with the Father, who sent me. In your own Law it is written that the testimony of two men is valid. I am one who testifies for myself; my other witness is the Father, who sent me.

—John 8:15-18

Study for the Day

These scriptures hit hard with me, because I realized that while I had forgiven my sister, I had never stopped judging her. We don't know why things happen, but we can know that God is in control and that all things work out for good. I had judged my sister all my life. I had always wanted to show her how to treat family and how to love. I wanted revenge, but "vengeance is mine" says the Lord (see Romans 12:19). I don't know why she left, but I chose to let it go and think of the wonderful gifts that God has blessed me with.

We have to stand guard against judging, for that same measure we use to judge will be used against us. It's hard, and I've gotten into a habit of trying to see others as God sees them. I try looking through a heart of compassion. I've found that if I don't judge others, they don't judge me as much. It's like that law of the universe: what we give, we get back. As I forgive and love others, others extend that same measure to me.

Galatians 6:7-9 says, "People reap what they sow. Those who sow to please their sinful nature, from that nature will reap destruction; those who sow to please the Spirit, from the Spirit will reap eternal life. Let us not become weary in doing good, for at the proper time we will reap a harvest if we do not give up." Is there anyone whom you've judged or falsely accused? As you meditate on these scripture today, ask that God to soften your heart and help you to see others the way He sees them.

_____

_____

_____

_____

_____

_____

_____

_____

_____

_____

_____

_____

_____

_____

_____

_____

_____

_____

_____

_____

_____

Day Five

A Brother Who Sins Against You

Scripture for the Day

If your brother sins against you, go and show him his fault, just between the two of you. If he listens to you, you have won your brother over. But if he will not listen, take one or two others along, so that "every matter may be established by the testimony of two or three witnesses." If they still refuse to listen, tell it to the church; and if they refuse to listen even to the church, treat them as you would a pagan or a tax collector.

—Matthew 18 15-17

Study for the Day

This one can be difficult when both you and the other person think you're right. Pray for direction. Try and help the other person understand your point of view in a loving way. Be courteous enough to listen to the other person's point of view. Work together in love to resolve any issues. Be thoughtful when you are giving tough feedback. Also, ask yourself how important the issue is to you. Try it; it makes a difference.

_____

_____

_____

_____

_____

_____

_____

_____

_____

No Condemnation

Scripture for the Day

Therefore, there is now no condemnation for those who are in Christ Jesus.

—Romans 8:1

"Condemnation" means to declare a person guilty or worthy of punishment. God alone is the judge. The mission of Christ was not to condemn, but to save the world. Because we have received a gracious pardon from God, we are directed to provide forgiveness to others. "Judge not, and you will not be judged" (Luke 6:37).

I had to decide to give up the right I thought I had to punish my sister. I had to stop condemning her. Furthermore, I didn't want God not to punish me for the things I had done and *deserved* to be punished for, so I had to extend that same pardon to others.

Study for the Day

If Christ's mission was to save the world and He has pardoned us, should we not be doing the same? How many pardons should you be extending? Today, meditate on Romans 8:1 and ask God to help you to stop condemning yourself and others.

_____

_____

_____

_____

_____

_____

_____

DAY SEVEN

Grace and Mercy

Thoughts for the Day

Two thoughts for this day. First, God's mercy and kindness are new every day. Second, we can come boldly to the throne of God and receive mercy and grace in our time of need.

"Mercy" is the aspect of God's love that causes Him to have compassion on you and not give you the punishment you deserve. In other words, mercy is what happens when you've completely messed up and done all kinds of wrong but God receives you and forgives you anyway. Instead of punishing you, He picks you up, brushes you off and sends you on your way. God shows compassion and mercy, and He expects us to be compassionate and merciful.

"Grace" is favor or kindness shown without regard for the merit or worth of the one who receives it, and it is given in spite of what that person actually deserves. In other words, grace is extending kindness and love to someone regardless of his or her actions—like Jesus when He gave up his life on the cross for us *despite* the fact that we were sinners.

Study for the Day

Starting today, focus on the things that God has given you that you don't deserve. Think of all the little blessings you take for granted—those unexpected things you were not looking for but greatly appreciated when you received them.

_____

_____

_____

_____

_____

_____

No Revenge

Scripture for the Day

A man's wisdom gives him patience; it is to his glory to overlook an offense.

—Proverbs 19:11

Do not say, "I'll do to him as he has done to me; I'll pay that man back for what he did."

—Proverbs 24 29

Do not take revenge, my friends, but leave room for God's wrath, for it is written: "It is mine to avenge; I will repay," says the Lord.

—Romans 12:19

Study for the Day

Because my heart was so hardened, it has taken me a number of years to learn to let things roll off my back and not be so easily offended. I also found on my journey to forgiveness that I had to let go of my desire to have my day of revenge. As we mature in Christ, we realize we are all flawed, and as we gain greater wisdom, we learn that we don't have to respond to something that offends us when it's not necessary. We have to trust that God will deal with the offense.

_____

_____

_____

_____

_____

_____

_____

Day Nine

Love for Enemies

Scripture for the Day

You have heard that it was said, "Love your neighbor and hate your enemy." But I tell you: Love your enemies and pray for those who persecute you, that you may be sons of your Father in heaven. He causes his sun to rise on the evil and the good, and sends rain on the righteous and the unrighteous. If you love those who love you, what reward will you get?

—Matthew 5:43-46

Study for the Day

It is easy for us to love our friends. There is no effort in that. Our friends make us laugh and smile, and we want to be around the things that bring us joy. But to love those who have hurt us takes courage. It takes real effort and a conscience decision to do so.

Over the course of my life, I have had a tendency to shut out the people who hurt me. As I said, it was my way of protecting myself. This was the behavior I displayed s a child. As a result, I created a lonely world for myself.

Jesus loved those who persecuted Him, and He has called us to a higher level in which we are no longer children in our relationship with God but are sons and daughters. It is through this higher level of relationship with Him that we demonstrate our maturity by displaying characteristics of Christ and loving those whom have caused us pain.

_____

_____

_____

_____

_____

_____

DAY TEN

Love, for the Day Is Near

Scripture for the Day

> Let no debt remain outstanding, except the continuing debt to love one another, for he who loves his fellowman has fulfilled the law. The commandments, "Do not commit adultery," "Do not murder," "Do not steal," "Do not covet," and whatever other commandment there may be, are summed up in this one rule: "Love your neighbor as yourself." Love does no harm to its neighbor. Therefore love is the fulfillment of the law.
>
> —Romans 13:8-10

Study for the Day

One day, a friend and I were talking about this commandment to "love your neighbor as yourself," and her comment was that most people don't know how to love themselves, let alone their neighbor. We talked that day about how to love yourself and summed it as follows: Do unto yourself as you would want others to do unto you. Be kind to yourself, forgive yourself, encourage yourself (even when no one else will), learn that you are important, invest in you. Then give that same loving care you gave to yourself to others.

Today, make a commitment to be good to yourself and to others. Write down three things you can start doing to show love to yourself, and then write down three things you can start doing to show love to others.

_____

_____

_____

_____

_____

_____

_____

DAY ELEVEN

Facing Trials

Scripture for the Day

Consider it pure joy, my brothers and sisters, whenever you face trials of many kinds [not *if* trials come, but *whenever* trials come], because you know that the testing of your faith produces perseverance (Italics added).

—James 1:2-3

Study for the Day

It took me a while to get to the place where I understood this scripture. As I look back, I realize that the experiences I've had made me who I am. God has a plan for each of us, and our experiences are part of it. When I admit it, I have learned from the trials I have been through, and as a result I have grown.

Today, look back at some of the trials you've experienced and think about the lessons and growth you've experienced as a result.

_____

_____

_____

_____

_____

_____

_____

_____

_____

_____

_____

Compassion, Kindness, Gentleness and Patience

Scripture for the Day

Therefore, as God's chosen people, holy and dearly loved, clothe yourselves with compassion, kindness, humility, gentleness and patience. Bear with each other and forgive one another if any of you has a grievance against someone. Forgive as the Lord forgave you. And over all these virtues put on love, which binds them all together in perfect unity.

—Colossians 3:12-14

Study for the Day

We are all accountable for our actions before God. As you reflect on your life, can you say that you've taken every opportunity to show compassion, kindness, gentleness and patience? Make a list of things or areas in your life where you think you can improve at showing compassion, kindness, humility, gentleness and patience. Pick your greatest area of weakness, and then choose to turn over a new leaf today.

_____

_____

_____

_____

_____

_____

_____

_____

_____

Day Thirteen

The Root of Bitterness

Scripture for the Day

See to it that no one misses the grace of God and that no bitter root grows up to cause trouble and defile many.

—Hebrews 12:15

Study for the Day

The root of bitterness is a small seed that can grow into a tree the size of a great oak tree if we allow it. We have to make the choice not to allow an offense to take root. We have to make the choice not continue to replay our hurts over and over again in our minds. That's the mistake I made: Day after day, I replayed the fact that my sister left me until the root of bitterness grew so deep it became a part of me.

What are you still bitter about? Take a moment to think about it. Then make the choice to let it go.

_____

_____

_____

_____

_____

_____

_____

_____

_____

_____

Unwholesome Talk

Scripture for the Day

Do not let any unwholesome talk come out of your mouths, but only what is helpful for building others up according to their needs, that it may benefit those who listen. And do not grieve the Holy Spirit of God, with whom you were sealed for the day of redemption. Get rid of all bitterness, rage and anger, brawling and slander, along with every form of malice. Be kind and compassionate to one another, forgiving each other, just as in Christ God forgave you.

—Ephesians 4:29-32

Study for the Day

This scripture sums up a lot of my past sins. You might say, "that's not so bad," but my attitudes were not pleasing to God. I was bitter with the world, and because I turned my bitterness within, it affected my life and others in many ways.

It is important for us to know how to handle our anger and not allow it to hurt others. It is not a sin to feel anger, but we have to be careful about how we respond to those feelings. In Ephesians 4:26, Paul says, "In your anger do not sin: Do not let the sun go down while you are still angry." We need to act immediately to resolve any issues when they come up; otherwise, we can give Satan an opportunity to cause strife and division in our lives.

Today, think about your attitude. Are you filled with encouragement that build others up and nurtures lasting relationships? Do you act in love? Are your words and actions pleasing to God?

_____

_____

_____

_____

_____

DAY FIFTEEN

Jesus Forgives Those Who Betray and Crucify Him

Scripture for the Day

While he was still speaking a crowd came up, and the man who was called Judas, one of the Twelve, was leading them. He approached Jesus to kiss him, but Jesus asked him, "Judas, are you betraying the Son of Man with a kiss?"…

The men who were guarding Jesus began mocking and beating him. They blindfolded him and demanded, "Prophesy! Who hit you?" And they said many other insulting things to him…

At daybreak the council of the elders of the people, both the chief priests and the teachers of the law, met together, and Jesus was led before them. "If you are the Messiah," they said, "tell us."

Jesus answered, "If I tell you, you will not believe me, and if I asked you, you would not answer. But from now on, the Son of Man will be seated at the right hand of the mighty God."

They all asked, "Are you then the Son of God?"

He replied, "You say that I am."

Then they said, "Why do we need any more testimony? We have heard it from his own lips…"

But with loud shouts they insistently demanded that he be crucified, and their shouts prevailed. So Pilate decided to grant their demand. He released the man who had been thrown into prison for insurrection and murder, the one they asked for, and surrendered Jesus to their will…

Jesus said, "Father, forgive them, for they do not know what they are doing." And they divided up his clothes by casting lots. The people stood watching, and the rulers even sneered at him. They said, "He saved others; let him save himself if he is God's Messiah, the Chosen One."

—Luke 22:47-48,63-71; 23:23-25,34-35

Study for the Day

This is the greatest example of forgiveness. Jesus asked God to forgive those who were about to kill him.

In the Old Testament, God accepted animal sacrifices for the forgiveness of sin. But these sacrifices did not remove sin. In the New Testament, there was a new covenant (a binding contract) between God and man. Jesus would die in the place of sinners. The blood of Jesus (God) would wash away the sins of all who believed.

Judas had agreed to point out Jesus to the crowd. The identifying signal was a kiss. It was a kiss of betrayal. Jesus was arrested and turned over for trial. The crowed mocked Him and demanded His death.

Even through Jesus endured pain beyond what we could ever comprehend, He was willing to die for our sins. Further, He asked God to forgive those who crucified Him for what they did. If Jesus can ask that His murderers be forgiven, shouldn't we be able to forgive those who have wronged us?

Have you ever had someone do something hurtful to you? Do you remember thinking, *I'll never forget what they've done to me*? Reflect on this. Be totally honest with yourself. Then make a choice to forgive those unforgivable things. Make a commitment today to make this a new way of life.

_____

_____

_____

_____

_____

_____

_____

_____

_____

_____

_____

Day Sixteen

Esau Forgives Jacob

Scripture for the Day

And Esau ran to meet him, and embraced him, and fell on his neck, and kissed him: and they wept.

—Genesis 33:4

Study for the Day

Read Genesis 27–33. This passage tells the story of Isaac and his two sons, Jacob and Esau. In the story, Jacob did the unthinkable. He knew that his father was going to bless Esau, so he disguised himself as Esau and stole his brother's birthright. When Esau found out, he began plotting to kill him. Jacob, fearing for his life, fled away.

More than twenty years passed. During this time, God began working to change Jacob from a manipulator into a man who leaned on God. The day was coming for Jacob and his brother to reunite. Jacob was afraid that Esau would still want to take revenge on him and his family for what he had done, so he sent a messenger ahead with a peace offering.

As Jacob prayed, he realized that God was his only hope. Jacob's "old man" would have tied to solve his problems on his own, but the "new man" wanted to solve his problems God's way. That night, Jacob was alone when a man appeared. Jacob wrestled with the man until daybreak, refusing to let him go until he blessed him (see Genesis 32:22-32). He was striving to have all God's blessing in his life.

As they wrestled, the man/angel touched the socket of Jacob's hip, which broke him. This was the final stage of removing Jacob's old nature. Jacob was now in a place of complete brokenness and surrender. No longer would he walk in his own strength. He would now have to lean on a cane, which was symbolic of his leaning on God alone.

This final act of God in Jacob's life was celebrated with a new name: Israel. No longer would Jacob strive with God or man. The process was now complete, and God could bless him abundantly. He gave him favor with Esau and restored their broken relationship. When Jacob reconciled with Esau, his brother greeted him with a hug—an incredible gesture, considering that he had once plotted to kill Jacob.

We must realize that our relationships are more important than the hurt we have experienced. When we do, we will go the extra mile to heal the bitter wounds. Today, can you think of how God has worked in your life to remove your old nature to a point of surrender in which you had to rely totally on Him?

_____

_____

_____

_____

_____

_____

_____

_____

_____

_____

_____

_____

_____

_____

_____

_____

_____

_____

_____

_____

DAY SEVENTEEN

Joseph Forgives His Brothers

Scripture for the Day

Now therefore be not grieved, nor angry with yourselves, that ye sold me hither: for God did send me before you to preserve life. For these two years hath the famine been in the land: and yet there are five years, in the which there shall neither be earing nor harvest. And God sent me before you to preserve you posterity in the earth, and to save your lives by a great deliverance. So now it was not you that sent me hither, but God: and he hath made me a father to Pharaoh, and Lord of all his house, and a ruler throughout all the land of Egypt. Haste ye, and go up to my father, and say unto him, Thus saith thy son Joseph, God hath made me Lord of all Egypt: come down unto me, tarry not: And thou shalt dwell in the land of Goshen, and thou shalt be near unto me, thou, and thy children, and thy children's children, and thy flocks, and thy herds, and all that thou hast: And there will I nourish thee; for yet there are five years of famine; lest thou, and thy household, and all that thou hast, come to poverty. And, behold, your eyes see, and the eyes of my brother Benjamin, that it is my mouth that speaketh unto you. And ye shall tell my father of all my glory in Egypt, and of all that ye have seen; and ye shall haste and bring down my father hither. And he fell upon his brother Benjamin's neck, and wept; and Benjamin wept upon his neck. Moreover he kissed all his brethren, and wept upon them: and after that his brethren talked with him… .

And Joseph said unto them, Fear not: for am I in the place of God? But as for you, ye thought evil against me; but God meant it unto good, to bring to pass, as it is this day, to save much people alive. Now therefore fear ye not: I will nourish you, and your little ones. And he comforted them, and spake kindly unto them.

—Genesis 45:5-15; 50:19-21, *KJV*

Study for the Day

Read Genesis 37–50. This passage tells the story of Joseph and his brothers, who sold him into slavery. As you read Joseph's story, notice that even through Joseph went through ordeal after ordeal, the favor of God was always upon him. Even in difficult situations, he acted with high integrity and acknowledged his need for God. Eventually, he went from being a slave to second in command in Egypt. As you read the story, notice how Joseph responded to his circumstances. Each time he said, "What shall I do now, Lord?" He was always looking for direction from God.

Today, think about some of the things people have done to you to hurt you. As you reflect on these situations, can you see God's hand at work, turning things in your favor?

_____

_____

_____

_____

_____

_____

_____

_____

_____

_____

_____

_____

_____

_____

_____

_____

_____

_____

_____

DAY EIGHTEEN

Moses Forgives the Israelites

Scripture for the Day

And Miriam and Aaron spake against Moses because of the Ethiopian woman whom he had married: for he had married an Ethiopian woman.

And they said, Hath the LORD indeed spoken only by Moses? hath he not spoken also by us? And the LORD heard it.

(Now the man Moses was very meek, above all the men which were upon the face of the earth.)

And the LORD spake suddenly unto Moses, and unto Aaron, and unto Miriam, Come out ye three unto the tabernacle of the congregation. And they three came out.

And the LORD came down in the pillar of the cloud, and stood in the door of the tabernacle, and called Aaron and Miriam: and they both came forth.

And he said, Hear now my words: If there be a prophet among you, I the LORD will make myself known unto him in a vision, and will speak unto him in a dream.

My servant Moses is not so, who is faithful in all mine house.

With him will I speak mouth to mouth, even apparently, and not in dark speeches; and the similitude of the LORD shall he behold: wherefore then were ye not afraid to speak against my servant Moses?

And the anger of the LORD was kindled against them; and he departed.

And the cloud departed from off the tabernacle; and, behold, Miriam became leprous, white as snow: and Aaron looked upon Miriam, and, behold, she was leprous.

And Aaron said unto Moses, Alas, my Lord, I beseech thee, lay not the sin upon us, wherein we have done foolishly, and wherein we have sinned.

Let her not be as one dead, of whom the flesh is half consumed when he cometh out of his mother's womb.

And Moses cried unto the LORD, saying, Heal her now, O God, I beseech thee.

—Numbers 12:1-13, *KJV*

Study for the Day

Miriam and Aaron, Moses' sister and brother, took issue with Moses because he had married an Ethiopian woman. They began to speak against him and question whether it was true that he alone heard from God. "Hath he not spoken also by us?" they asked.

As punishment for their actions, God afflicted Miriam with leprosy. Yet even though Miriam and Aaron had harbored ill will in their hearts toward Moses and spoken hurtful things against him, he asked God to heal his sister.

There are several lessons here. First, when you have an issue with someone, be honest about it and try to resolve the problem peacefully and in love. Second, recognize that your ill feelings can cause hurt to others. And third, forgive those who have hurt you.

_____

_____

_____

_____

_____

_____

_____

_____

_____

_____

_____

_____

DAY NINETEEN

David Forgives Saul

Scripture for the Day

He came to the sheep pens along the way; a cave was there, and Saul went in to relieve himself. David and his men were far back in the cave. The men said, "This is the day the LORD spoke of when he said to you, 'I will give your enemy into your hands for you to deal with as you wish.'" Then David crept up unnoticed and cut off a corner of Saul's robe.

Afterward, David was conscience-stricken for having cut off a corner of his robe. He said to his men, "The LORD forbid that I should do such a thing to my master, the LORD's anointed, or lay my hand on him; for he is the anointed of the LORD." With these words David sharply rebuked his men and did not allow them to attack Saul. And Saul left the cave and went his way.

Then David went out of the cave and called out to Saul, "My lord the king!" When Saul looked behind him, David bowed down and prostrated himself with his face to the ground. He said to Saul, "Why do you listen when men say, 'David is bent on harming you?' This day you have seen with your own eyes how the LORD delivered you into my hands in the cave. Some urged me to kill you, but I spared you; I said, 'I will not lay my hand on my lord, because he is the LORD's anointed.' See, my father, look at this piece of your robe in my hand! I cut off the corner of your robe but did not kill you. See that there is nothing in my hand to indicate that I am guilty of wrongdoing or rebellion. I have not wronged you, but you are hunting me down to take my life. May the LORD judge between you and me. And may the LORD avenge the wrongs you have done to me, but my hand will not touch you. As the old saying goes, 'From evildoers come evil deeds,' so my hand will not touch you."

—1 Samuel 24:3-13

Study for the Day

Saul was the man whom God appointed to be king of Israel. He was known for his courage and generosity, but as his power grew, so did his pride. Eventually, he no longer sought God for direction.

God rejected Saul as king of Israel and sent his prophet Samuel to anoint a boy named David to be the next king (see 1 Samuel 16). David, like everyone else, had his strengths and weaknesses, but he was later remembered for having a heart for God (see Acts 13:22).

Saul grew jealous of David because of his popularity and attempted to kill him. Now, had this been one of us, we would have wanted to take revenge against Saul. But David never laid a hand on him.

There is so much violence and hatred in the world today. Just think of how our neighborhoods would change if we chose not to take revenge on those whom we thought deserved it.

_____

_____

_____

_____

_____

_____

_____

_____

_____

_____

_____

_____

_____

_____

_____

_____

_____

_____

DAY TWENTY

The Stoning of Stephen

Scripture for the Day

When they heard this, they were furious and gnashed their teeth at him.

But Stephen, full of the Holy Spirit, looked up to heaven and saw the glory of God, and Jesus standing at the right hand of God.

"Look," he said, "I see heaven open and the Son of Man standing at the right hand of God."

At this they covered their ears and, yelling at the top of their voices, they all rushed at him, dragged him out of the city and began to stone him. Meanwhile, the witnesses laid their clothes at the feet of a young man named Saul.

While they were stoning him, Stephen prayed, "Lord Jesus, receive my spirit."

Then he fell on his knees and cried out, "Lord, do not hold this sin against them." When he had said this, he fell asleep.

—Acts 7:54-60

Study for the Day

Each time I study the Word of God, I gain new understanding. The story of Stephen is so powerful, yet one that I don't hear talked about as much. Stephen was known as a wise servant. So that you may experience the fullness of who he was and what his death represented, go back and read Acts 6.

A group called the Synagogue of the Freedmen (see Acts 6:9) lied regarding Stephen, causing dissension among the people. They accused him of blasphemy (the same thing that Jesus had been accused of in Matthew 25). The crowd grew angry, and they dragged Stephen outside the city and began to stone him. Even as they did this, he asked God to forgive them.

Are you willing to share your faith with others, even if they turn away?

DAY TWENTY-ONE

Love One Another

Scripture for the Day

This is the message you heard from the beginning: We should love one another. Do not be like Cain, who belonged to the evil one and murdered his brother. And why did he murder him? Because his own actions were evil and his brother's were righteous. Do not be surprised, my brothers, if the world hates you. We know that we have passed from death to life, because we love our brothers. Anyone who does not love remains in death. Anyone who hates his brother is a murderer, and you know that no murderer has eternal life in him. This is how we know what love is: Jesus Christ laid down his life for us. And we ought to lay down our lives for our brothers. If anyone has material possessions and sees his brother in need but has no pity on him, how can the love of God be in him? Dear children, let us not love with words or tongue but with actions and in truth. This then is how we know that we belong to the truth, and how we set our hearts at rest in his presence whenever our hearts condemn us. For God is greater than our hearts, and he knows everything.

—1 John 3:11-15

Study for the Day

Read the story of Cain and Abel in Genesis 4:1-16. Abel found favor with God by honoring him with his first fruits, while Cain offered what was left over. When God rejected Cain's sacrifice, he killed his brother out of jealousy and anger. This was the first murder in the Bible. All Cain had to do to correct the situation and his relationship with God was to repent and start doing what was right.

The Word says that we are to help our brother, yet so many of us have hatred in our hearts toward one another. I know my heart was full of hatred for my sister.

Think of similar situations that you have been faced with in your life. Did you make the choice to change, or did you continue on the same path? Will you make the choice to change and do what is right, or will you continue to do what is wrong?

_____

_____

_____

_____

_____

_____

_____

_____

_____

_____

_____

_____

_____

_____

_____

_____

_____

_____

_____

_____

_____

_____

_____

Committing Murder in Your Heart

Scripture for the Day

You have heard that it was said to the people long ago, "You shall not murder, and anyone who murders will be subject to judgment." But I tell you that anyone who is angry with a brother or sister will be subject to judgment. Again, anyone who says to a brother or sister, "Raca," is answerable to the Sanhedrin. And anyone who says, "You fool!" will be in danger of the fire of hell.

Therefore, if you are offering your gift at the altar and there remember that your brother or sister has something against you, leave your gift there in front of the altar. First go and be reconciled to that person; then come and offer your gift.

Settle matters quickly with your adversary who is taking you to court. Do it while you are still together on the way, or your adversary may hand you over to the judge, and the judge may hand you over to the officer, and you may be thrown into prison. Truly I tell you, you will not get out until you have paid the last penny.

—Matthew 5:21-26

Study for the Day

This scripture will probably hit home with a lot of people. Not only are we not to commit murder, but we are also not to get so angry that we want to murder. But pay attention, because this is questioning the condition of your heart. In your heart, are you guilty of murder?

_____

_____

_____

_____

_____

_____

DAY TWENTY-THREE

More than Physical Healing

Scripture for the Day

And Jesus went about all Galilee, teaching in their synagogues, and preaching the gospel of the kingdom, and healing all manner of sickness and all manner of disease among the people. Then His fame went throughout all Syria; and they brought to Him all sick people who were afflicted with various diseases and torments, and those who were demon-possessed, epileptics, and paralytics; and He healed them.

—Matthew 4:23-24

Study for the Day

Jesus had three main aspects of his ministry: preaching, teaching and healing. His healings teach us His concern for our wholeness. His miracles of healing help to substantiate His teaching and preaching (His power) and establish that He was the Son of God.

Note in the passage above that Jesus healed "diseases and torments." To me, this demonstrates that His healing was also for the spirit and emotions. I have learned that there is nothing (sin or sickness) too small or large for God, and when I put my burdens before Him and trust Him, there is nothing He won't do for me.

Studying the Word of God shows us that Jesus offers hope, peace and eternal life. What is it that you are missing in your life?

_____

_____

_____

_____

_____

_____

DAY TWENTY-FOUR

Jesus Forgives and Heals a Paralytic

Scripture for the Day

So He got into a boat, crossed over, and came to His own city. Then behold, they brought to Him a paralytic lying on a bed. When Jesus saw their faith, He said to the paralytic, "Son, be of good cheer; your sins are forgiven you."

And at once some of the scribes said within themselves, "This Man blasphemes!"

But Jesus, knowing their thoughts, said, "Why do you think evil in your hearts? For which is easier, to say, 'Your sins are forgiven you,' or to say, 'Arise and walk'? But that you may know that the Son of Man has power on earth to forgive sins"—then He said to the paralytic, "Arise, take up your bed, and go to your house." And he arose and departed to his house.

Now when the multitudes saw it, they marveled and glorified God, who had given such power to men.

—Matthew 9:1-8

Study for the Day

As we study the healing power of Jesus, we will often see Him perform physical healings. But in this passage, Jesus is more concerned with forgiving the paralytic man's sins. As I studied on, I discovered that both the man's body and spirit were paralyzed, because not only was he sick physically but he also didn't know Jesus. Healing the man's spirit was Jesus' first priority. Forgiving his sins gave the man hope, and it also helped the man know who Jesus was.

_____

_____

_____

_____

Jesus Heals a Great Multitude

Scripture for the Day

And Jesus went about all Galilee, teaching in their synagogues, preaching the gospel of the kingdom, and healing all kinds of sickness and all kinds of disease among the people. Then His fame went throughout all Syria; and they brought to Him all sick people who were afflicted with various diseases and torments, and those who were demon-possessed, epileptics, and paralytics; and He healed them. Great multitudes followed Him—from Galilee, and from Decapolis, Jerusalem, Judea, and beyond the Jordan.

—Matthew 4:23-25

Study for the Day

As we study the healing miracles of Jesus Christ, I can't help but reflect on how many times God has healed me and my family. My uncle had prostate cancer, but he has had a good PSA level for years. At seventy-eight, God brought him through a five artery bypasses. While patients in the rooms next door didn't make it, no trouble came to his door.

We know that it was only by the grace of God. Today, take the time to reflect on how God has healed you or someone in your family.

DAY TWENTY-SIX

Jesus Cleanses a Leper

Scripture for the Day

When He had come down from the mountain, great multitudes followed Him. And behold, a leper came and worshiped Him, saying, "Lord, if You are willing, You can make me clean."

Then Jesus put out His hand and touched him, saying, "I am willing; be cleansed." Immediately his leprosy was cleansed.

And Jesus said to him, "See that you tell no one; but go your way, show yourself to the priest, and offer the gift that Moses commanded, as a testimony to them."

—Matthew 8:1-4

Study for the Day

In some cultures, lepers and persons with diseases considered incurable were sometimes sent away so that others would not get sick. But Jesus was able to cure the incurable. In this story, the leper had faith and asked Jesus to heal him. What illness have you been suffering from? Jesus is able to cure the incurable. Ask Jesus if He is willing to heal you.

_____

_____

_____

_____

_____

_____

_____

_____

_____

Jesus Heals a Centurion's Servant

Scripture for the Day

Now when Jesus had entered Capernaum, a centurion came to Him, pleading with Him, saying, "Lord, my servant is lying at home paralyzed, dreadfully tormented."

And Jesus said to him, "I will come and heal him."

The centurion answered and said, "Lord, I am not worthy that You should come under my roof. But only speak a word, and my servant will be healed. For I also am a man under authority, having soldiers under me. And I say to this one, 'Go,' and he goes; and to another, 'Come,' and he comes; and to my servant, 'Do this,' and he does it."

When Jesus heard it, He marveled, and said to those who followed, "Assuredly, I say to you, I have not found such great faith, not even in Israel! And I say to you that many will come from east and west, and sit down with Abraham, Isaac, and Jacob in the kingdom of heaven. But the sons of the kingdom will be cast out into outer darkness. There will be weeping and gnashing of teeth." Then Jesus said to the centurion, "Go your way; and as you have believed, so let it be done for you." And his servant was healed that same hour.

—Matthew 8:5-13, *NKJV*

Study for the Day

From this passage we see that the centurion was a man of power, but he realized that he did not have the ability to heal his servant. Jesus was amazed at the faith the centurion showed, and as a result He healed his servant "that same hour." We must not put our faith in people just because they have power. We must realize that the only one who can heal us is Jesus.

_____

_____

_____

_____

Day Twenty-Eight

Peter's Mother-in-Law Healed

Scripture for the Day

Now when Jesus had come into Peter's house, He saw his wife's mother lying sick with a fever. So He touched her hand, and the fever left her. And she arose and served them.

—Mathew 8:14-15

Study for the Day

Here again, Jesus performs another miracle of healing. However, what I want you to focus on today is what Peter's mother-in-law did immediately after Jesus healed her. *She got up and began to serve Him.* She was so grateful Jesus healed her that she wanted to serve Him.

This is the same overwhelming gratitude I feel each time I think about who God is and what He has done for me. I want to serve Him. Jesus didn't have to bless me in the many ways that He has, but I am so glad He did, and out of my gratitude I want to serve Him. Are you serving or doing anything as a result of what God has done for you?

_____

_____

_____

_____

_____

_____

_____

_____

_____

Many Healed in the Evening

Scripture for the Day

When evening had come, they brought to Him many who were demon possessed. And He cast out the spirits with a word, and healed all who were sick, that it might be fulfilled which was spoken by Isaiah the prophet, saying: "He Himself took our infirmities and bore our sicknesses."

—Matthew 8:16-17

Study for the Day

Read this passage and focus on what you have studied about the healing miracles of Jesus. Concentrate on His compassion. Think of His power. All He had to do was speak, and His word healed. The Word of God is powerful. Let it speak into your life.

_____

_____

_____

_____

_____

_____

_____

_____

_____

_____

_____

_____

DAY THIRTY

Two Demon-Possessed Men Healed

Scripture for the Day

When He had come to the other side, to the country of the Gergesenes, there met Him two demon-possessed men, coming out of the tombs, exceedingly fierce, so that no one could pass that way. And suddenly they cried out, saying, "What have we to do with You, Jesus, You Son of God? Have You come here to torment us before the time?"

Now a good way off from them there was a herd of many swine feeding. So the demons begged Him, saying, "If You cast us out, permit us to go away into the herd of swine."

And He said to them, "Go." So when they had come out, they went into the herd of swine. And suddenly the whole herd of swine ran violently down the steep place into the sea, and perished in the water.

—Matthew 8:28-32

Study for the Day

Demons are fallen angels who have joined forces with Satan in rebellion against God. In this scripture, they wanted to know what Jesus wanted with them before the appointed time. In Revelation 20:10, it says that the devil will be thrown into a lake of burning sulfur. The demons knew their fate; they just wanted to know why Jesus was there before it was time. They knew that Jesus had the power to cast out demons, and they asked to be sent into the heard of pigs. Again, Jesus just said "go," and the demons obeyed Him. How powerful.

So, what do you see here? The demons' mission was to destroy, but Jesus loved the demon-possessed man and drove the demons out of him. It's not a hard choice. Will you follow Someone who loves you and values your life, or someone who wants to destroy you?

_____

_____

_____

Day Thirty-One

Made in God's Image

Scripture for the Day

And God said, "Let us make man in our image, after our likeness: and let them have dominion over the fish of the sea, and over the fowl of the air, and over the cattle, and over all the earth, and over every creeping thing that creepeth upon the earth." So God created man in his own image, in the image of God created he him; male and female created he them.

—Genesis 1:26-27, *KJV*

For You formed my inward parts; You covered me in my mother's womb. I will praise You, for I am fearfully and wonderfully made.

—Psalm 139:13-14, *NKJV*

For we are His workmanship, created in Christ Jesus for good works, which God prepared beforehand that we should walk in them.

—Ephesians 2:10, *NKJV*

To the praise of the glory of His grace, by which He made us accepted in the Beloved.

—Ephesians 1:6, *NKJV*

Study for the Day

Although we will never be totally like God because He is a supreme creator, we can choose to reflect His image through love, patience, forgiveness, kindness and faithfulness. Are you reflecting the image of God? In which of these five areas are you strong, and in what areas do you need to improve?

Knowing that I was made in God's image allowed me to begin to understand who I was and helped me realize what I was worth to Him. It made me stop putting myself down, because I realized that I was criticizing what God had created.

Think of the ways you are criticizing God's work, and then ask God to forgive you for sinning against Him. Create an attitude of thankfulness in your heart for all He has done.

_____
_____
_____
_____
_____
_____
_____
_____
_____
_____
_____
_____
_____
_____
_____
_____
_____
_____
_____
_____
_____
_____
_____
_____

DAY THIRTY-TWO

"I AM"

Scripture for the Day

And Moses said unto God, Behold, when I come unto the children of Israel, and shall say unto them, "The God of your fathers hath sent me unto you; and they shall say to me, What is his name? what shall I say unto them?"

And God said unto Moses, "I AM THAT I AM": and he said, "Thus shalt thou say unto the children of Israel, I AM hath sent me unto you."

—Exodus 3:13-14, *KJV*

Study for the Day

Read Exodus 3. Moses wanted the people to know who God was, and he asked God for His name. "I AM" was the name God used to describe His power and character. I AM, the God who appeared to Moses, is the same God who lives today. Our God is a God who speaks and acts.

One way to share who God is with others is to tell them what He has done for you. Everyday make it a point to share what God has done for you with someone else. Keep a journal of your blessings as a reminder during hard times.

_____

_____

_____

_____

_____

_____

_____

_____

DAY THIRTY-THREE

God's Protection

Scripture for the Day

Do not be terrified by them, for the LORD your God, who is among you, is a great and awesome God.

—Deuteronomy 7:21

Know therefore that the LORD your God is God; he is the faithful God, keeping his covenant of love to a thousand generations of those who love him and keep his commands.

—Deuteronomy 7:9

Wherefore say unto the children of Israel, "I am the LORD, and I will bring you out from under the burdens of the Egyptians, and I will rid you out of their bondage, and I will redeem you with a stretched out arm, and with great judgments."

—Exodus 6:6

For God so loved the world, that he gave his only begotten Son, that whosoever believeth in him should not perish, but have everlasting life.

—John 3:16

Study for the Day

Our Creator has promised to never leave us, so we can be assured that He will always be with us, and we do not have to be afraid. God is great; He is awesome. Just look at His creations all around you.

God is a protector, a provider and a deliverer. What burdens do you need God to bring you out from under? In what areas are you in bondage? Are their some habits or wrong thought patterns that need to be broken? (If we are honest, I think all of us would have to answer yes to that last question.)

How has God protected you? How has He provided for you? I'll share a story with you to show one way in particular that He protected me. One morning, I got up and had a cup of tea while reading my devotion for the day. I rushed to get dressed and get to work. I forgot that the flame under the tea kettle was still on, and I left the house. When I returned, the flame was still burning under the tea kettle. It was a miracle that it was not scorched. I had been gone for twelve hours.

The most important verse for you to remember is John 3:16, that God loves us so much that He sacrificed His son's life for us. This is the verse that taught me about love. As I grew in love, I began to disregard what I wanted and put others' needs before mine. For when we love freely, we are willing to give as God has so freely given to us.

_____

_____

_____

_____

_____

_____

_____

_____

_____

_____

_____

_____

_____

_____

_____

_____

_____

_____

_____

DAY THIRTY-FOUR

More than Conquerors

Scripture for the Day

No, in all these things we are more than conquerors through him who loved us. For I am convinced that neither death nor life, neither angels nor demons, neither the present nor the future, nor any powers, neither height nor depth, nor anything else in all creation, will be able to separate us from the love of God that is in Christ Jesus our Lord.

—Romans 8:37-39

Study for the Day

Jesus has said that we are more than conquerors in all these things: trouble, hardship, persecution, famine, nakedness, danger and the sword. What areas of your life do you need to conquer?

_____

_____

_____

_____

_____

_____

_____

_____

_____

_____

_____

Blessings for Obedience

Scripture for the Day

If you fully obey the LORD your God and carefully follow all his commands I give you today, the LORD your God will set you high above all the nations on earth. All these blessings will come upon you and accompany you if you obey the LORD your God:
You will be blessed in the city and blessed in the country.

The fruit of your womb will be blessed, and the crops of your land and the young of your livestock—the calves of your herds and the lambs of your flocks.

Your basket and your kneading trough will be blessed.

You will be blessed when you come in and blessed when you go out.

The LORD will grant that the enemies who rise up against you will be defeated before you. They will come at you from one direction but flee from you in seven.

The LORD will send a blessing on your barns and on everything you put your hand to. The LORD your God will bless you in the land he is giving you.

The LORD will establish you as his holy people, as he promised you on oath, if you keep the commands of the LORD your God and walk in his ways. Then all the peoples on earth will see that you are called by the name of the LORD, and they will fear you. The LORD will grant you abundant prosperity—in the fruit of your womb, the young of your livestock and the crops of your ground—in the land he swore to your forefathers to give you.

The LORD will open the heavens, the storehouse of his bounty, to send rain on your land in season and to bless all the work of your hands. You will lend to many nations but will borrow from none. The LORD will make you the head, not the tail. If you pay attention to the commands of the LORD your God that I give you this day and carefully follow them, you will always be at the top, never at the bottom. Do not turn aside from any of the commands I give you today, to the right or to the left, following other Gods and serving them.

—Deuteronomy 28:1-14

Study for the Day

God has promised to give us blessings for obedience. What's stopping you today from receiving your blessings?

_____

_____

_____

_____

_____

_____

_____

_____

_____

_____

_____

_____

_____

_____

_____

_____

_____

_____

_____

_____

_____

Day Thirty-Six

Foolish or Wise?

Scripture for the Day

Reckless works pierce like a sword but the tongue of the wise brings about healing.

—Proverbs 12:18

Study for the Day

Proverbs teaches us wisdom, and knowing God is key to our being wise. Because a large part of this study is about choices, let's look at a few characteristics of the wise.

The Foolish Man	The Wise Man
Ignores God	Seeks to know God
Is reckless in deed and words	Chooses to heal in deed and words
Is a know-it-all	Accepts correction and guidance
Ignores instruction	Accepts criticism and instruction

Think about some of the choices you have made. Are they foolish or wise? Proverbs 10:1 says, "A wise son brings joy to his father, but a foolish son grief to his mother." When you make a mistake, are you big enough to accept correction and learn from your mistakes? Or are you full of pride, not willing to accept criticism or instruction? Proverbs 16:18 states, "Pride goeth before destruction, and an haughty spirit before a fall" (*KJV*). Are you headed for destruction?

_____

_____

_____

_____

_____

The Whole Armor of God

(Part One)

Scripture for the Day

Finally, my brethren, be strong in the Lord and in the power of His might. Put on the whole armor of God, that you may be able to stand against the wiles of the devil. For we do not wrestle against flesh and blood, but against principalities, against powers, against the rulers of the darkness of this age, against spiritual hosts of wickedness in the heavenly places. Therefore take up the whole armor of God, that you may be able to withstand in the evil day, and having done all, to stand.

Stand therefore, having girded your waist with truth, having put on the breastplate of righteousness, and having shod your feet with the preparation of the gospel of peace; above all, taking the shield of faith with which you will be able to quench all the fiery darts of the wicked one. And take the helmet of salvation, and the sword of the Spirit, which is the word of God; praying always with all prayer and supplication in the Spirit, being watchful to this end with all perseverance and supplication for all the saints—and for me, that utterance may be given to me, that I may open my mouth boldly to make known the mystery of the gospel, for which I am an ambassador in chains; that in it I may speak boldly, as I ought to speak.

—Ephesians 6:10-20

Study for the Day

The armor of God is the defense (and, in some cases, the offense) of the Christian. Without it, the enemy can gain access to our lives. To be victorious in our battles, we must rely on God's strength and use our armor. (Truth is, apart from God, we don't have any strength). Our whole body must be protected, leaving no part vulnerable. And even though we have been assured victory, we must fight until the return of Jesus. For it is Satan's job to keep us from a right relationship with God.

Where are you vulnerable, and how are those vulnerabilities keeping you from having a right relationship with God?

_____

_____

_____

_____

_____

_____

_____

_____

_____

_____

_____

_____

_____

_____

_____

_____

_____

_____

_____

_____

_____

_____

_____

_____

The Whole Armor of God

(Part Two)

Study for the Day

Today, I wanted to share more on the armor of God so that we can all learn how to apply each piece.

Piece of Armor	Characteristic	Function
Belt	Truth	Satan is a master at manipulation. Sometimes, he fights with lies that sound like the truth. God's truth enables us to be on guard so that we will recognize and defeat Satan's lies.
Breastplate	Righteousness	The breastplate covers the heart. My heart was attacked early in life through my emotions. As a result, I spent far too many years being bitter. Always protect your heart.
Footgear	Share the Word	God wants us to share the Word. The footgear is our willingness to take the Word of God to those who don't know Him.
Shield	Faith	The shield protects us from the fiery darts of the enemy. Without faith, it's impossible to please God. We have been called to walk by faith, not by sight.

Piece of Armor	Characteristic	Function
Helmet	The Word	The helmet protects us from attacks to the mind. Satan plants seeds of doubt that cause us to turn from God. We must keep our focus on God.
Sword	The Spirit/Word	We will encounter difficult times throughout the course of our lives, but when we are tempted, we have to trust in God's Word.

_____

_____

_____

_____

_____

_____

_____

_____

_____

_____

_____

_____

_____

_____

_____

_____

_____

Day Thirty-Nine

Real Love

Scripture for the Day

If I speak in the tongues of men and of angels, but have not love, I am only a resounding gong or a clanging cymbal. If I have the gift of prophecy and can fathom all mysteries and all knowledge, and if I have a faith that can move mountains, but have not love, I am nothing. If I give all I possess to the poor and surrender my body to the flames, but have not love, I gain nothing.

Love is patient, love is kind. It does not envy, it does not boast, it is not proud. It is not rude, it is not self-seeking, it is not easily angered, it keeps no record of wrongs. Love does not delight in evil but rejoices with the truth. It always protects, always trusts, always hopes, always perseveres.

Love never fails. But where there are prophecies, they will cease; where there are tongues, they will be stilled; where there is knowledge, it will pass away. For we know in part and we prophesy in part, but when perfection comes, the imperfect disappears. When I was a child, I talked like a child, I thought like a child, I reasoned like a child. When I became a man, I put childish ways behind me. Now we see but a poor reflection as in a mirror; then we shall see face to face. Now I know in part; then I shall know fully, even as I am fully known. And now these three remain: faith, hope and love. But the greatest of these is love.

—1 Corinthians 13:1-13

For God so loved the world that he gave his one and only Son, that whoever believes in him shall not perish but have eternal life. For God did not send his Son into the world to condemn the world, but to save the world through him. Whoever believes in him is not condemned, but whoever does not believe stands condemned already because he has not believed in the name of God's one and only Son.

—John 3:16-18

Study for the Day

I couldn't end my fast without studying what God said about love. So today, I want to focus on what real love is all about. This Scripture describes how much God loves us. Focus for a moment on the phrase "for God so loved the world." This means *you and me.* "That he gave his one and only son." This means all we have to do is *choose* to believe in Christ, and we will have eternal life. God sent His Son into the world that we might be saved through Him. How can you reject His gift of salvation?

_____

_____

_____

_____

_____

_____

_____

_____

_____

_____

_____

_____

_____

_____

_____

_____

_____

_____

_____

_____

_____

_____

_____

DAY FORTY

Final Instructions

Scripture for the Day

Now we ask you, brothers, to respect those who work hard among you, who are over you in the Lord and who admonish you. Hold them in the highest regard in love because of their work. Live in peace with each other. And we urge you, brothers, warn those who are idle, encourage the timid, help the weak, be patient with everyone. Make sure that nobody pays back wrong for wrong, but always try to be kind to each other and to everyone else.

Be joyful always; pray continually; give thanks in all circumstances, for this is God's will for you in Christ Jesus.

Do not put out the Spirit's fire; do not treat prophecies with contempt. Test everything. Hold on to the good. Avoid every kind of evil.

May God himself, the God of peace, sanctify you through and through. May your whole spirit, soul and body be kept blameless at the coming of our Lord Jesus Christ. The one who calls you is faithful and he will do it.

Brothers, pray for us. Greet all the brothers with a holy kiss. I charge you before the Lord to have this letter read to all the brothers.

The grace of our Lord Jesus Christ be with you.

—1 Thessalonians 5:12-28

CONCLUSION
A NEW CREATURE

CONGRATULATIONS ON COMPLETING this journey. I hope that you have enjoyed this time of discovery and fellowship and that in the course of forgiving you have learned how to love God's way. I pray that the new creature in you will continue on the path of developing a relationship with God. With the completion of this book comes renewal of your spirit, a change in your identity and the way you think and act.

Don't be disappointed if you don't recognize your change right away. Keep walking; it's coming. In fact, it's already done. When you accept Jesus as Savior and Lord of your life, the Holy Spirit will rise up in you, and therefore you will have everything you need. It's just a matter of having what's on the inside show up on the outside.

As for me, I can't go back to the old way I used to live, and because of this choice, my life will never be the same. I thank God for what He has done. He has healed my past and present, and because of the Lord, I know I have a wonderful future. Remember the introduction to the Kirk Franklin CD that I hated so much? Now I pray "that I will become a great woman of God and that this book will be used for His glory."

I close this book with a toast. First, praise and honor to God for loving me even when I didn't deserve it. Second, a toast to myself, for having the courage to be honest with myself, admit my weaknesses, forgive and to let go of the past.

As I close an old chapter in my life and move forward to a new beginning, I could hear the Holy Spirit whisper, "By my stripes you are healed and made whole. *You are made whole.*" And if you listen to His voice, let go of your hurt and forgive others, you will be made whole as well.

Printed in the United States
149505LV00008B/1/P